Arts and Crafts Collection

Beginning Tatting: A Lesson Book

Atheen Wilson

O Pine Press

All rights reserved. No part of this book may be reproduced, stored in a retrieval system or transmitted in any form or by any means, electronic, mechanical, photocopied, recorded or otherwise, without prior written permission of the author except for brief quotes and illustrations used for review purposes.

ISBN1452859329
EAN-139781452859323
Primary Category: Crafts & Hobbies / General
Country of Publication: United States
Language: English
Search Keywords: Tatting; Lace; Shuttle made lace; Fiber Arts; Tatting Lessons
Contributors: Authored by Atheen Wilson, photos by the author, tatting done by the author

O Pine Press

O Pine Press
803 Huron St SE
Mpls, MN
55414

© 2010, Atheen Marie Wilson

To Pati O'Brien
For encouraging me to press on with the project.

Contents

Contents	**vii**
Introduction	**11**

Part One: Chains — 21

Lesson 1:   Hands and how to use them to tat   23
     Purpose: Learning the double stitch

Lesson 2:   Chains   33
     Project: Chain necklace for a focal pendant.
     Purpose: Learn to make a chain
                    Continue to practice the double stitch (ds)

Lesson 3:   Picots   39
     Project: Chain bracelet of picots (p) and double stitches (ds)
     Purpose: Learn to make the picot (p)
                    Learn to read a pattern
                    Practice the double stitch

Lesson 4:   Joining chains for elaboration   47
     Project: Necklace of two or more chains joined (j) to one another with picots
     Purpose: Learn to join (j) chains to one another by the means of picots
                    Continue to practice the double stitch (ds) and picot (p)
                    Practice reading a pattern

Lesson 5:   The chain as motif—the "reverse work" instruction   55
     Project: Square or diamond chain motif
     Purpose: Learn the "reverse work" instruction
                    Continue to practice the double stitch (ds) and picot (p)
                    Practice reading a pattern

Lesson 6:   Adding beads to your tatting   65
     Project: Bracelet of double stitches and beads.
     Purpose: Learn to add beads to a tatted design
                    Continue to practice the double stitch (ds) and picot (p)
                    Practice reading a pattern

Part Two: Rings — 71

Lesson 7:   Rings--breaking away from the "signals"   73
     Project: Single rings for an edging (kitchen towel)

	Purpose:	Learn to make rings
		Practice the double stitch (ds) and picot (p) on the shuttle thread
		Practice reading a pattern

Lesson 8:   **Joining rings**   **81**
     Project: Rings joined in threes for an edging (holiday hand towel)
     Purpose: Learn to join rings
                 Practice the double stitch (ds) and picot (p) in rings
                 Practice reading a pattern

Lesson 9:   **Avoiding the thread spaces**   **91**
     Project: Rings with chains joining motifs
     Purpose: Learn to use a chain to join motifs
                 Learn about adding threads
                 Learn how to vary a pattern
                 Practice joining rings
                 Practice reading a pattern

Lesson 10:   **Alternate treatment of thread spaces—interweaving threads**   **99**
     Project: Bookmark with interwoven threads
     Purpose: Learn to use shuttle "weaving" to join motifs
                 Practice reading a pattern

Lesson 11:   **Joining rings into a circle—the double twist**   **105**
     Project: Daisy earrings, pin, boutonniere, or bouquet
     Purpose: Learn to join an end ring with a first ring to complete a round motif

Lesson 12:   **Adding beads to rings**   **113**
     Project: Daisy with beads
     Purpose: Learn to add beads to rings in two methods

Lesson 13:   **Joining individual motives—longer and larger projects**   **121**
     Project: Joined motifs
     Purpose: Learn to join motifs into larger projects

Part Three: Details   129

Lesson 14:   **Putting it all together**   **131**
     Purpose: Learn to create more elaborate patterns using chains and ring motifs

Lesson 15:   **Reading other styles of pattern instructions**   **159**
     Purpose: Learn to interpret different styles of instructions in familiar terms

Lesson 16:   **Starching your creations and other ideas**   **163**

Appendices **169**
    Suggested uses for tatted edgings and motifs   **171**
    Decision list: the creative bit   **172**
    Tatting books   **173**
    Form for samples and notes   **175**

Bibliography **177**

About the author **181**

Introduction

Me, Myself and I

I learned to tat comparatively "late" in life. While I had already started knitting by age 5 with the help of my mother, who was an adept and avid knitter, and crocheting by age 8 with my grandmother, who preferred it to knitting, I didn't learn to tat until I was 18.

I was intrigued by tatting and decided to learn how to do it, because I had seen examples of it on antique handkerchiefs and hand decorated stationery. It was light and lovely and much lacier looking than the knitted and crocheted laces I had also seen. Some of the craft books that provided instructions and patterns for other fiber arts also featured tatted lace for edgings and medallions that were well and truly impressive, and I'd collected a number of them even before I had learned to actually do them.

I'd tried tatting numerous times by studying the craft books that included a few instructions, but I usually gave it up as futile after coming up with a series of useless knots over and over again. Not until an older friend of my mother's noted my efforts and offered me a hand did I succeed at last.

It was my own difficulties in trying to learn tatted lace by written instruction, however, that convinced me that it was by no means an "easy" task to learn from a book, at least not as they were written at the time. I have not had occasion to change my opinion on the subject over the years, either, since almost all of the tatted lace books I've collected, while providing stellar patterns, also seem to assume the purchaser already knows how to tat. Certainly the instructions seem perfunctory at best.

I decided to write my own book on the subject in a way that would not only show the learner how to do it right, but also point out where they might go wrong, so they could more effectively correct their method. In short I will harvest my own bounty of goof-ups to foresee student problems before they occur. I also hope to provide a series of lessons and projects that will help the student learn by actually doing projects which become more elaborate with each lesson, until the entire process of tatted lace is learned and understood. Thus, by completing the entire series of lessons, the student should understand all of the facets involved in tatting and perform any pattern they come upon in other books on the subject. Even if the student stops at any given stage, they will take away something useful about the methods. The more advanced the stopping point is, the greater the versatility the student will possess in doing his or her own projects. Even mastery of the first chapter may be enough for some individuals to "catch on" and go on to more advanced pattern books.

What's So Difficult about It?

Yes; just what *is* so difficult about tatting anyway? You'd be surprised. It's all in how our brains work and how we use our hands because of it. In fact, if I were to come up with a good antidote for Alzheimer's, it would be some form of training that encouraged the use of the hands in a different way than the individual's usual.

For many beginners the biggest difficulty in learning tatted lace is simply knowing which thread to pull. Pull the right one, and you achieve your goal of slip stitches (which is what the double stitch is); pull the wrong one, and you end up with a series of useless, immoveable knots. Most learners come up with those loathsome knots.

This should come as no surprise. Most people are right hand dominant; that is they do most active things with their right hand and tend to "think" with it. The function of the left is left merely to assist the right.[1] So much is this the case that we often don't quite know what the left hand has been doing—hence the old saying that the right hand doesn't know what the left is doing.[2] In tatting, however, the left hand is the working hand, the one the tatter needs to "think with." While the right hand has its own tasks, the left is the one actually performing the knotting action.

> *In Tatted Lace, the lace maker's hands become a "machine" upon which lace is made.*

For most of us, crocheting and knitting are fairly straight forward, with obvious stitches performed mostly by the right hand. With practice one becomes easily proficient. This is not the case with tatted lace and, since a continuous stream of intractable knots is frustrating and discouraging, is primarily why many people give up and also why tatting is rapidly becoming a lost art.

Tatting, like playing a musical instrument requires the practitioner to train both hands to do simultaneous but different things. Anyone who has ever tried to

---

[1] With the left hand dominant, the reverse is true.
[2] One day while I was in college I was busy writing a term paper, and my left hand, entering into the spirit of the moment, picked up a letter from my mother it was my intention to read later and put it safely aside. That much I remembered. What I couldn't recall was *where* I had put it. I found it nearly a decade later tucked into a book I'd briefly consulted while writing the paper at the time!

learn the piano or the guitar knows exactly what I mean. Here, too, the right and left hands have their own individual tasks to perform in order to produce the goal of music and avoid the calamity of noise.

In tatting, once each hand has learned its own tasks, the entire process is quite simple; with even the most elaborate pattern, there is only one main stitch, the double stitch. Like the double half-hitch in animal husbandry, climbing and boating, and the lark's head in macramé, the tatted double stitch is intended to slide easily over the thread on which it's based. Once the hands have learned it, it becomes automatic and requires almost no thought beyond counting out the number of double stitches needed to create the pattern. Essentially the lace maker's hands become a "machine" upon which lace is made.

Materials and Equipment
Fibers

Tatting, like other fiber arts, uses a variety of yarns, threads and other cords. It can be made with the finest linen, silk, wool, cotton or synthetic threads or with bailing twine or rope. The limits on gauge are set by the dexterity of the tatter's hands and by the size of shuttle he or she can handle. Obviously, the size of the fiber used will influence the size and character of the object produced. I have used the same pattern to make a tatted snowflake in size 20 crochet thread, in nylon cord, and in macramé twine. The first project was about five inches in diameter and used a standard tatting shuttle; the second was about seven or eight inches across and used a Tatsy shuttle; while the latter was at least a foot and a half across and required a handmade cardboard bobbin.

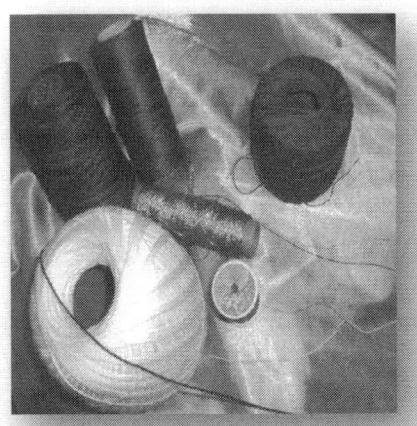 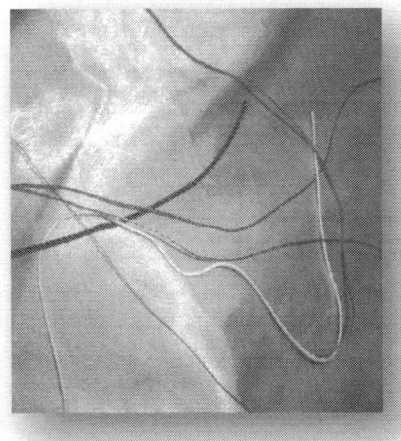

Threads (left) and Thread Sizes (right)

Needless to say, the uses for the three were quite different. The first was a Christmas tree ornament, the second a stain proof doily for a heavily used outdoor table, and the latter a small rug for a balcony.

Selection of your working material will be determined by your ultimate goal. If you want to make a few tatted flowers with which to decorate a note card, sewing thread would be a perfect choice. It comes in an amazingly wide variety of colors and creates a very light and lacy look. There is at least one book, *Tatting Collage*[3], that deals almost entirely with this type of use, illustrating a variety of motifs with which to create your cards.

Christmas ornaments can be made in white or colored crochet threads, which are readily available in craft stores and on the internet. Slightly heavier cords, in silver or gold, and embroidery floss in gold, silver, copper, and other colors of metallic threads, will also make attractive ornaments and splendid jewelry chains and mounts. Floss in other colors can be used to make chains and other motifs for decorating clothing and other wearable items. Again, the proposed use for the tatted item will determine the choice of material.

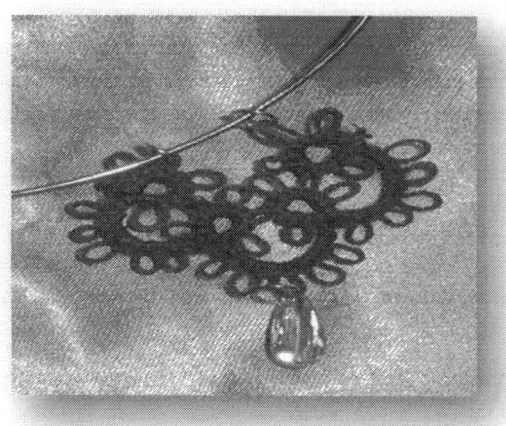

Tatted Medallion Necklace in Green Crochet Thread with Peridot Crystal Pendant

Synthetic lines make stain resistant objects. "Rat tail," "mouse tail" and "bug tail" sized satin cords[4] make splendid motifs of various sizes for decorating clothing, furniture and other items. In short, if it comes in a flexible, linear form, you can probably tat with it. I've even used dental floss to tat.

---

[3] Lindsay Rogers, *Tatting Collage*, Sterling Press, 1996.

[4] I take no responsibility for the terminology, which comes from jewelry materials and certainly brings size to mind rather vividly.

Shuttles

The only other necessity in the practice of tatting is the *shuttle*. A shuttle is simply a hand held device which confines the fibers being used in a convenient fashion. The most commonly recognized use of a shuttle is in weaving. As with the weaving shuttle that for tatting is generally lozenge shaped. This facilitates its movements through the thread wound around the hand and the fingers of that hand. Coming in a variety of shapes, sizes, materials, and styles, each has a particular aspect that recommends it to the user. Some of the easiest to use are also the least expensive.

If it comes in a flexible, linear form, chances are you can tat with it.

The largest shuttle, known by the brand name Tatsy and about three or four times as large as the standard versions, holds a very large amount of thread of the most common sizes or a smaller amount of the larger cords. The former use makes completing a large and complicated motif with one length of thread much easier to do. This produces a smoother, more professional appearance, because there is no need for splices as the project is worked. Those who want to use larger gauges of fibers will find that the Tatsy will hold sufficient material to finish a project with no more frequent splices than one might have with a smaller shuttle with finer thread. Twine-sized fibers, however, are almost destined to be used on a hand-made bobbin of some kind, because even the Tatsy cannot hold sufficient amounts of this larger material.

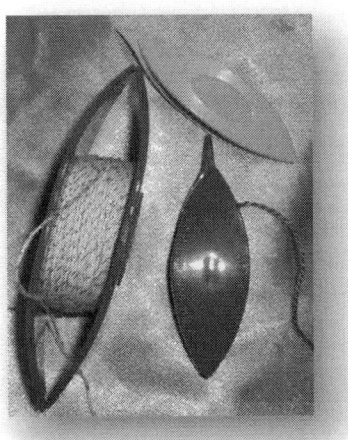

The Tatsy Shuttle with Two Smaller Plastic Shuttles

Plastic tatting shuttles have become the most common and least expensive. There are several types, some with a straight projection with which to undo knots and some with a slight curved projection for the same purpose. There is even a plastic shuttle with a small, metal "crochet hook" at the end. The shuttles come in three sizes, the largest, as mentioned already, is the Tatsy. The smallest is possibly the most comfortable in the hand, but it holds less thread and is not as easily used in actual practice as the shuttle only slightly larger.

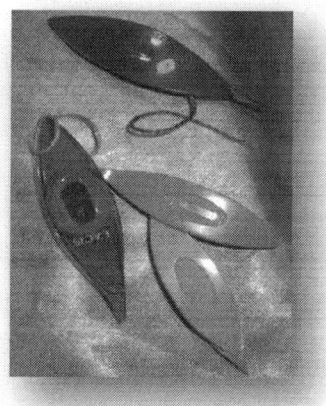

Colors and Shapes of Plastic Shuttles

All of these require patience in the winding process, since the two sides of the shuttle tend to come very close together at the point where the thread must pass through for this process. While this is a liability in the winding process, it is a strong point in the actual use of the shuttle since it prevents the thread with which it is wound from unwinding too easily during use. One can simply drop the shuttle if needed without worrying that it will unleash its entire contents.

Open Ends

Metal shuttles usually come with a separate bobbin, like that from a sewing machine. This pops out of the surrounding case so that the user can wind the thread more easily and quickly than he or she could with a plastic or other type of solid shuttle. Furthermore, several bobbins can be wound with the same thread making the addition of thread during a project much easier. Metal shuttles suffer from a certain "stiffness" in the process of unwinding thread during

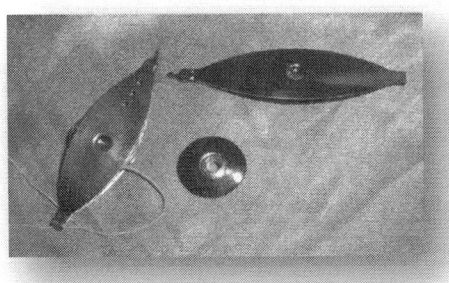

Metal Shuttles with Exposed Bobbin

tatting. I've even broken a fine sewing thread when trying to release more working thread. This accident arises from the friction between the moveable bobbin and the surrounding metal case. Paraffin wax can ease this tension, but oils should be avoided in order to prevent damage to the fibers on the bobbin or to the finished lace.

Shuttles also come in various wooden versions. Usually they are expensive and are produced primarily for those who enjoy esthetics. They are actually rather difficult to use, because the thread tends to escape easily from between the two halves by accident while resisting the same effort during work. Furthermore, winding the thread onto the shuttle can be very tedious. I have some in walnut, ebony, and rosewood, but I rarely use them; I enjoy having them because they're pretty.

**Wood Shuttles in Rosewood (left)
and Ebony (right)**

Sometimes antique shuttles can be found; again these can be very expensive depending upon their rarity and their age. These come in metal, bone, ivory, early forms of plastic, and wood. Some have inscriptions and dates on them. Again, the ease of their use is variable, and they are mostly objects for a collector.

Antique Metal Shuttle (probably late19th or early 20th Century) with Etched Design on the Sides

The History of Tatting

It is difficult to write a history of this craft, since few tatted objects or shuttles survive prior to those of the 19th century. This doesn't, however, mean that tatting could not have existed at an earlier age; only that if it did, it has left no earlier trace.

Some craft historians suggest that paintings from the 18th century may depict women tatting (most notably Charlotte of Mecklenburg-Strelitz, Madame Adelaide, the daughter of Louis XV of France and Anne, Countess of Albemarle). Others believe the shuttles the women held were part of a different craft called cord making.[5] It should be noted, however, that these women were members of the upper classes, not customarily active in household crafts except as they occurred as pastimes; if they were represented with tatting shuttles, it might be supposed that individuals of lesser status and therefore unlikely to have had their portraits painted, had been using them for far longer. As the common saying goes, absence of evidence is not evidence of absence.

My opinion is that the craft is really quite old, probably as old as net making, and was probably created by a fishing people. It may have been a male invention if it arose in a culture where men were responsible for this activity. The shuttle and the manner of its use bespeaks a people who understood both

---

[5] I suspect this is begging the question, since the technique was probably the same, and as I noted above, any fiber could be tatted.

knotting and net making. I actually saw shuttles somewhat larger than the Tatsy shuttle in use for this purpose in Malaga/Toromolinos, Spain in 1970, and by this time it would seem likely that these net making shuttles had been in use for generations.

Whenever it was invented and whether men or women invented it, tatting was destined for decorative motifs and household embellishment, and for lace makers became a professional cottage industry, by at least the 19th century. It was at this time that published works on tatting and patterns for use began to appear in Europe, and special tatting schools began to appear at least in England. Some of the finest and most elaborate tatted works that have survived date to the 19th century, when it was used for decorating women's and children's clothing and household items. Fine examples of these appear in museum collections in France, England, and Scandinavia.

Nineteenth century patterns and many from the first half of the 20th century are still available in tatting collections today and some are available in their original form from a variety of sources.[6] More recently tatting designs are dedicated to smaller projects like doilies, snowflakes, jewelry, and three dimensional ornaments like bells and balls, which fit into the limited time available for craft projects in the modern lifestyle than do those for table cloths, bedspreads, or table linens. Patterns for this type of use have become increasingly more available. A search of the internet will find books on the subject in Russian *(Плетение)*, French *(Frivolité)*, Italian *(Chiacchierino)*, German *(Spitzen-Kreationen)*, and Japanese, as well as in English[7].

---

[6] See the section below on Tatting Books.
[7] See the section below on Tatting Books.

PART ONE: Chains

Lesson 1: Hands and How to Use Them to Tat

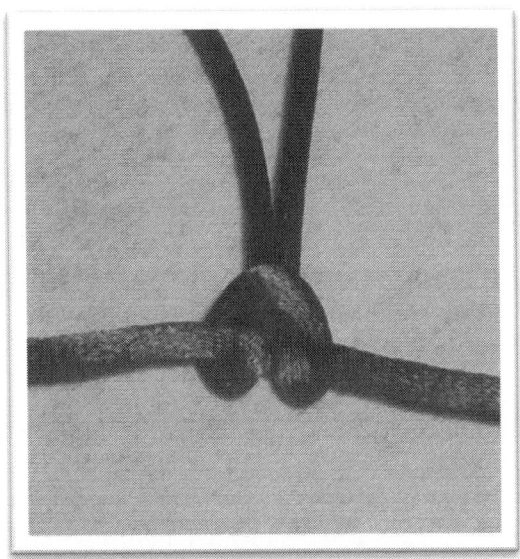

A Close-up of a Double Stitch in Rat Tail Cord (on a Ring)

Purpose: **Learning the double stitch (ds)**

Discussion:

Tatted lace is made by creating a series of *slip stitches* along a thread. These are generally made in left and right pairs and are called a *double stitch*. If the thread along which they are made is the same one that is used to make the double stitch itself, the product will be a *ring* of double stitches. If they are made with a second thread, referred to as the ball thread, the result will be an open *chain* of double stitches.

When properly made, the double stitch looks a little like the Greek letter pi (π) as in the above photo. It is the top bar of the π shape that is stitch "one," not the legs as "one, two." What the latter features are is the left and right hand sections of a completed double stitch.

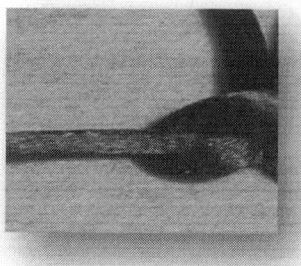 

A Close up of the Left and Right Half Stitches of a Completed Double Stitch

Half stitches are occasionally required in patterns—and are then indeed counted individually—but these are relatively rare instances and do not appear to be increasing in popularity. Doing a series of left or right half single stitches produces a twisting of the stitches to the left or to the right. A series of either in a heavier weight thread make a nice lanyard.

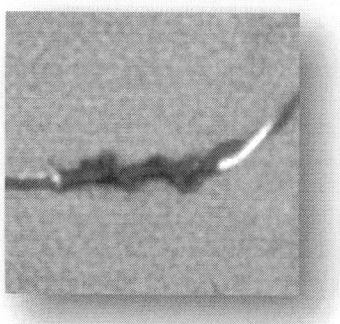

Twisting Half Stitches

While most people want to go directly to making the rings for which tatting is so noted, in fact the best place for them to begin is with *chains*. The reason for this is that, while rings are done on a single thread, chains require two, the ball and the shuttle threads. Because of this, the learner can use two different colors of thread, distinguishing the stitch making thread from the base thread. In the instance below, the ball thread is dark and the shuttle is white.

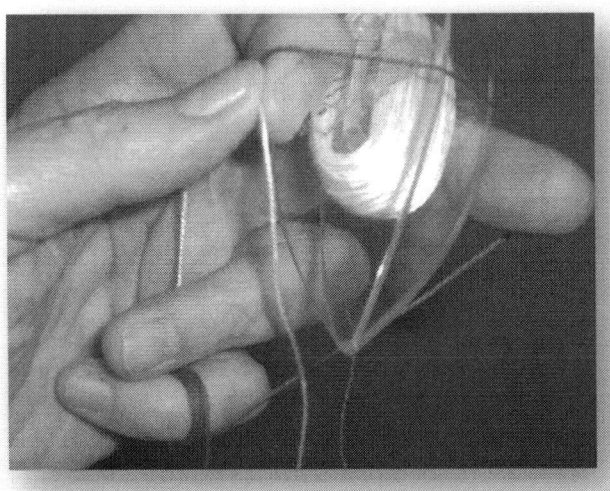

Two Different Colors Used to Make a Chain

Since it is the left hand or ball thread hand (here dark colored) that creates the double stitch itself, if the tatted chain is white, the tatter has made knots not slip stitches. In a properly made tatted chain, all the stitches would be dark in this instance, because the ball thread would be wrapped around the shuttle thread. The appearance of an incorrect color will immediately reveal the error, so the knot can be removed before an entire string of them have been made.

Below is a photograph of a properly made chain, with metallic ball thread and black cotton shuttle thread. All of the double stitches are metallic, and it is only where the tails of the finished chain are tied together that the black shuttle thread appears at all.

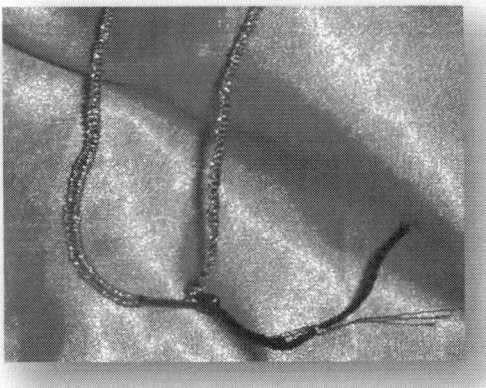

Tatted Chain Showing the Shuttle Threads in Black

To begin the lesson, you will tie the ball and shuttle threads together with an overhand knot. The resulting knot is then held between the left thumb and index finger:

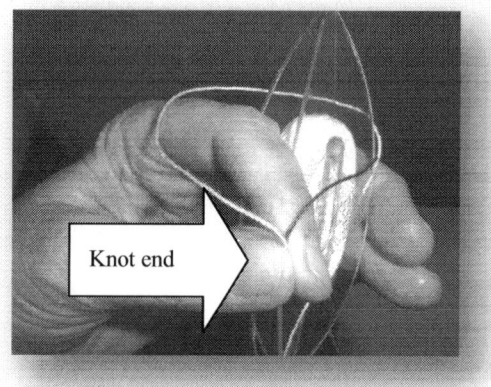

Knotted End

Next the ball thread, here again dark, is wrapped loosely around the back of the other four fingers and repeatedly around the little finger to anchor it.

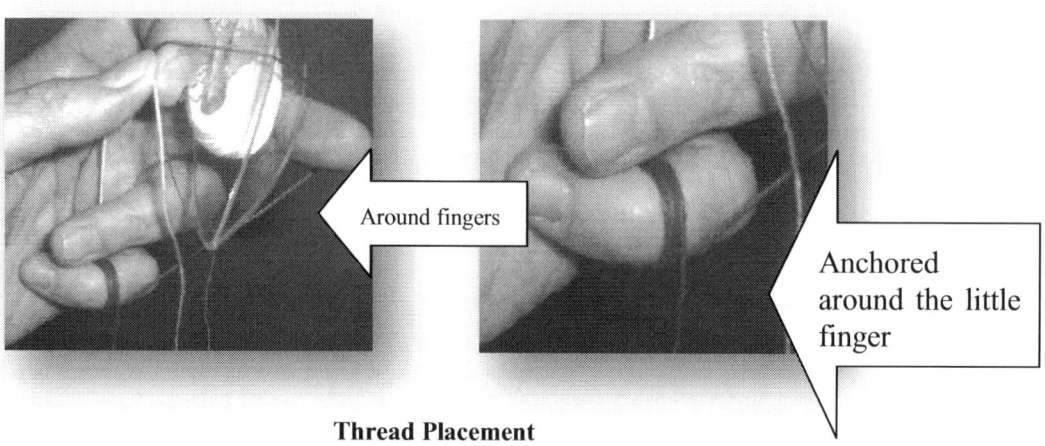

Thread Placement

As can be seen from the left hand photograph above, the dark thread, the ball thread, makes an arc rather than a complete circle around the back of the hand. It starts at the thumb and ends at the little finger.

With rings the same thread, the shuttle thread, would have passed loosely around the little finger as it did the others, making a return to the thumb and index finger where it would be stabilized along with the tail, completing a circle. In that case, the same thread would have made both the base and the stitches. With chains the white shuttle thread is the base over which the dark double stitches are created.

To begin the *first half of the double stitch*, you lay a loose loop of the shuttle thread in an upward position, across your left hand over the ball thread wrapped around it. The shuttle is then passed *up and between the threads* (here dark and white). The fingers of your left hand should be fairly relaxed at this point.

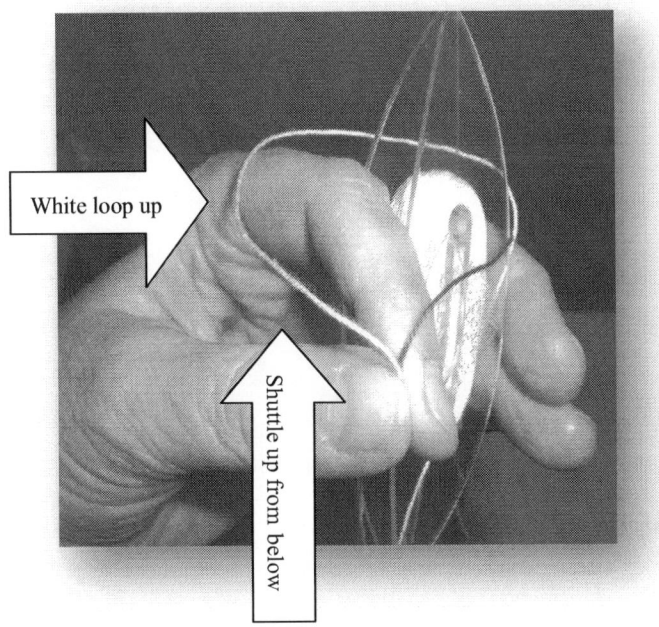

Shuttle Position for First Half of Double Stitch

At this point having cleared the fingers, your shuttle is then stretched taught against the restraining thumb and forefinger creating a firm base line of thread along which the double stitches can be formed with the ball thread.

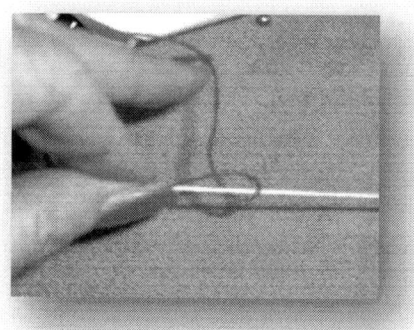

Taught Shuttle (Base) Thread and Loop of Ball Thread

The relaxed fingers of the left hand allow the loop to form naturally. In the photo below, the first half of the double stitch is light satin "mouse" tail cord on a base thread of black.

Forming the First Half of the Double Stitch

Notice here that the loop is curving *around and under the black* shuttle thread, then it travels *up and over the light* cord and away.

Remember as long as the fingers of your left hand are relaxed and the shuttle thread remains in a firm linear position, the ball thread will almost automatically form a small loop over the shuttle thread. By gently flexing the fingers of your left hand, the loop will gradually move up against the knot held between your thumb and index finger. This makes the first half of the π shaped double stitch.

Practice making these stitches, until you come to feel more comfortable with the procedure and with handling your shuttle and threads. Make certain you are seeing the correct color on the cord. If it's the wrong color, in this case the black cord, the stitches will not slide easily along the base thread. Even with chains there should be some degree of "play" along the base. If you find there isn't in your own samples, examine where you might have gone wrong and try again.

Notice that as you make your stitches, the finished product will start to turn to the left or away from you in a twist. You will see when you make the right hand or second half of the double stitch repeatedly, the product will turn to the right or toward you as you repeat the half stitches.

Perhaps make a length of cord long enough for a lanyard for a name tag or a set of keys. The second half of the double stitch is made in much the same way, so your practice at this point will much facilitate that step.

To make the *second half of the double stitch*, the loop of your shuttle thread is dropped into a downward position over the ball thread. This time the shuttle passes between the index finger and the other three from *above and down*:

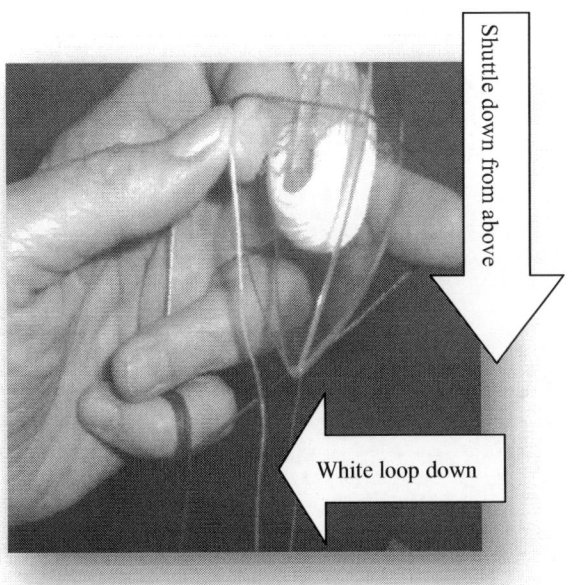

Thread position for second half of the Double Stitch

You will note that whereas the loop and shuttle were travelling up, now they are both travelling down. This is what produces the observed change in direction between the left and right hand parts of the double stitch.

If you examine the direction of the ball thread in the next photo, you will

Forming the Second Half of the Double Stitch

see that it travels *under and then over the black* shuttle thread, and *then beneath the lighter colored* mouse tail. This makes the right leg of the double stitch and also completes the cross section of the π.

Again, the fingers of your left hand remain relaxed while the shuttle thread is stretched taut by your right hand as it was in the previous instance. A loop almost automatically forms in the ball thread with this motion. With a simple manipulation of the fingers of the left hand, the loop will tighten, closing it toward the first half of the double stitch.

Compare the two halves of the double stitch in the photographs below and see how they relate to the completed double stitch on the far right:

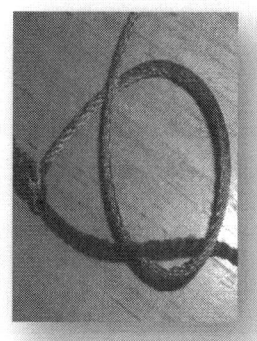 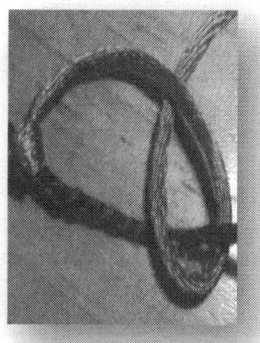 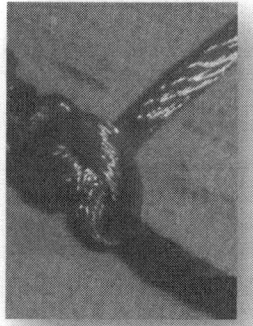

First and Second Halves of the Double Stitch and Completed Double Stitch

Now make a series of single right hand stitches as you did before. You might make another lanyard in a different colored thread. Save a sample of these two twisted cords, labeling them according to stitch type so that you can study them in the future should you want to make something employing these stitch types.

Again, make certain you are seeing the correct color on the cord. If it's the wrong color, the stitches will not slide easily along the base thread. Certainly depending upon the pattern, knots in chains might not make a great deal of difference to the outcome of your design, but once you start rings, knots will prevent you from closing them to create your motif.[8] If the ring stitches are knots, you won't be able to close the ring to make your motif. That's very frustrating, because you would have to undo all the knots and stitches back to the first mistake and redo the tatting to make the pattern work. It's better to learn proper stitches from the beginning to save yourself the frustration.

For those of you who have already tried tatting and found your efforts have not met with success, it is this fundamental process that probably caused your difficulties. You might like to take time out at this point in the lesson to take a look at your technique. Which thread are you pulling taut, the ball or the shuttle; and which hand are you using to loop the thread around the other? Right or left hand? If your knot slides, you're pulling the correct thread; if not, you aren't. It's that simple. Remember that when you are making a loop, the right hand remains inactive and the left does the work.

You will probably notice that the shuttle movement of the right hand feels much like pulling a needle away from sewing work in order to tighten a stitch in place. That feeling will be familiar to the hand sewer. If you have experience with sewing, embroidery or crewel, you should find your right hand will almost automatically assume its role in the tatting procedure if you think in these terms. The left hand is more mechanical in its actions.

Now practice *double stitches* using the two color method until you feel confident you understand the basic technique. In this instance you will make first one half and then the other half for a complete double stitch. Don't be surprised if you find it difficult; it *is* difficult. Once your hands have learned what to do, it'll become much easier, almost automatic. It really is your *hands* that must "understand" the process. Be patient. After this hurtle the rest is actually easy.

---

[8] Knots on a chain after a picot is made, however, will prevent the picot from forming because the knot will not slide over the base cord to close the space between the two double stitches that compose the picot. This will be explained further later.

It really is your hands that must "understand" the process. Be patient. After this one hurtle the rest is actually easy.

Lesson 2: Chains

Project: Chain necklace for a focal pendant.

Double Stitch Chain in Gold Cord

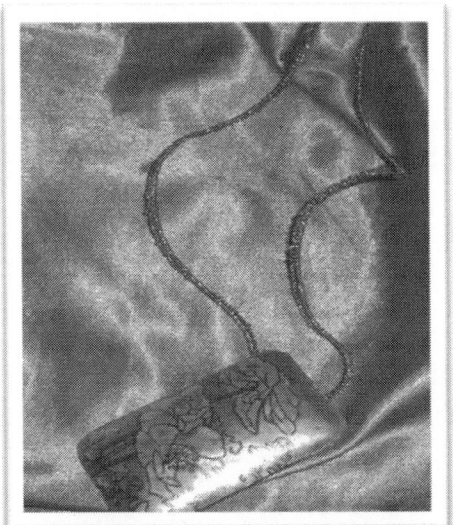

1. Long Chain with Cloisonné Pendant

2. Short Chain with a Triad of Dyed Coral Pendants

Purpose: Learn to make a chain
Continue to practice the double stitch (ds)
Materials: Crochet cotton or other thread in desired colors, any size (the illustration is in gold craft and black crochet cotton).
Tatting shuttle
Tape measure
Pendant or other ornament for the necklace (here a cloisonné pendant)
Jewelry findings if needed: clasp, crimp pin cover, head- or eye-pins, jump-rings, etc.
Glue adhesive
Scissors
Jewelry pliers if needed
Length: As desired, generally 18" or longer.

Discussion:

Chains by themselves are useful for jewelry and other projects. They can also be an important aspect of more complex tatting patterns, since they allow ring motifs to be connected to one another in more elaborate fashions. While simple rings can be connected by lengths of thread, this usually ends with attempts to hide or disguise them in various ways. Chains make these rouses unnecessary as you can see by the two photos below:

 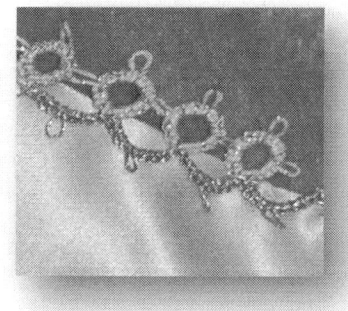

Connections between Rings: without Chains (left) and with Chains (right)

Chains can also be decorative in and of themselves. A simple chain can be used as a necklace, or it can be rolled into various shapes and sewn together to make decorations for clothing and household items. Several chains can be braided, with chains of different colors combining to produce a variety of effects, especially in jewelry projects. With the introduction of the picot in Lesson 3, chains can also be connected to one another (below left) or to other parts of themselves (below right) to create more elaborate motifs.

 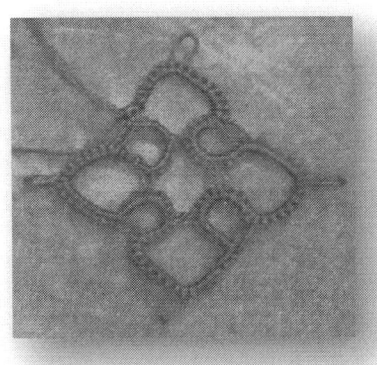

Uses for Chains

Purpose:

By the time you've completed this project, you should be an expert at the double stitch and the chain. Your stitches should be more uniform and even, and there should be no stray loops above the row of stitches.[9] The completed stitches should move smoothly over your shuttle thread. The latter is important for the next lesson.

Pattern:

First:
1. Tie two different colors of thread together, a ball in one color and a shuttle in another. Choose for the shuttle the color you wish to *hide*. The chain you produce should look the color of your ball thread.
2. Hold the knot between the thumb and index finger of the left hand and pass the ball thread over the outsides of the remaining fingers, looping

---

[9] Loops above the stitches have a place in tatted design; in fact, they're called picots, but small irregular and unintended loops should be avoided.

3. Using your shuttle thread, position a large *loop up and over* the tops of the left hand fingers and pass the *shuttle up from below and between* the two colors of threads through the arc created by the three outer fingers.
4. Pull the *shuttle away* from your work to tighten the shuttle thread. It will feel a little like a sewing motion.
5. Keep this thread taught while you use the fingers of your left hand to *make a loop* with the ball thread and gently nudge it closed and against the knot held in the thumb and index finger.

First half of your double stitch is completed. Check to make certain that your stitch is the color of the *ball thread* and that it is lying over the shuttle thread.

Next:
1. Make a loop of the shuttle *thread down* from your fingers.
2. Pass the *shuttle down from above* and between the shuttle and ball threads.
3. Draw the shuttle thread taught *away* from the work in your left hand.
4. Gently nudge the loop of the ball thread close to the first half of the double stitch.

Second half of the double stitch completed.

Make an entire series of double stitches, until you have a chain of a comfortable length for a necklace. If you find that you have made a knot, use the point of your shuttle, if there is one, or a crochet hook or other pointed object to loosen the knot. Pass the shuttle through the threads until the knot is removed, then replace it with a correct double stitch. Tie off and cut the thread from the ball and shuttle threads, leaving a length for finishing as below.

Finishing:

Add a pendant or some other type of focal to the chain, if desired, using a head- or eye-pin and jump-ring if needed. Add a clasp to either end of the chain, or tie the ends together. If the latter, glue the knot with craft glue and cut the remaining ends. Cover the knot with a crimp cover.

Note:

In completing this project, you should not only learn how to do the double stitch correctly, you should also attempt to make them even. Leaving gaps of the thread between halves of the stitches or between them makes the work look uneven and ragged. It's not that this is "wrong," but it's not definitely "right" either unless it was your intention to introduce texture to the design. Technique is important, and making an effort to produce smooth, even, stitches is part of it. For most patterns, proper technique produces better results. If you begin designing your own patterns, adding texture by varying your technique can produce interesting and useful detail in the motif. The difference in this instance, however, is *control*.

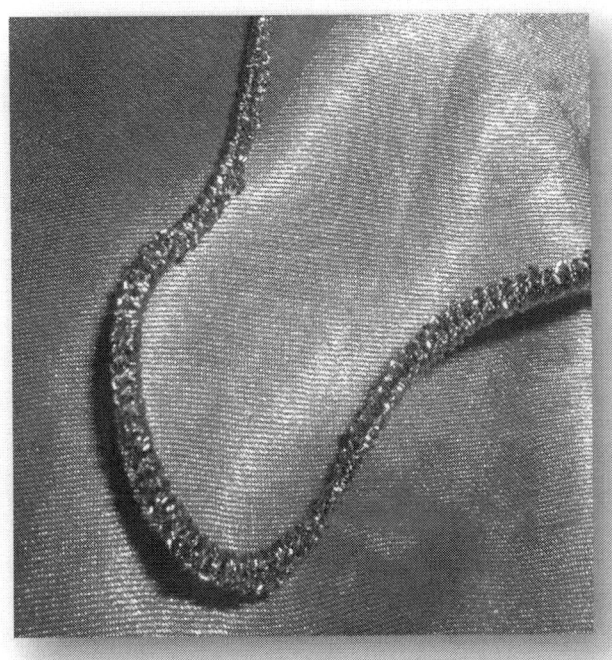

Tatted Chain with Even Double Stitches

Technique is important, and making an effort to produce smooth even stitches is part of it.

Lesson 3: Picots

Project: Chain bracelet of picots (p) and double stitches (ds)

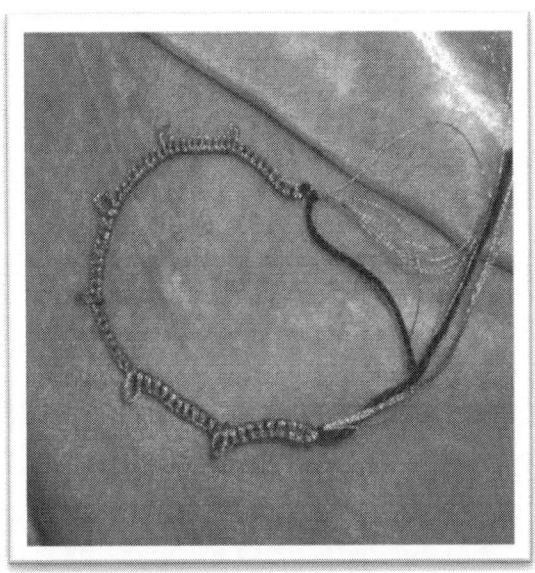

Bracelet in Copper Embroidery Floss with Double Stitches and Picots

Purpose: Learn to make the picot (p)
Learn to read a pattern
Practice the double stitch

Materials: Crochet cotton, synthetic or satin lines, or embroidery floss in choice of colors.
Tatting shuttle
Measuring tape
Pendant or other ornaments if desired
Jewelry findings if needed: clasp, crimp cover, head- or eye-pins, jump-rings, etc.
Glue adhesive
Scissors
Jewelry pliers if required

Length: As needed to fit the wrist if a clasp is added or long enough to pass over the widest part of the hand with thumb tucked in if tied.

Discussion:

By the time you have finished this project your hands will have become much more automatic in their production of double stitches. Knots will have become less frequent, the stitches will be more uniform in appearance, and you will more accurately count the individual π shapes.

This project introduces the *picot*, one of the most important structures in tatting. Here it is in its simplest form, that of decoration. Later projects will introduce its other uses.

With this lesson too, you will start reading a pattern as they are usually published in tatting pattern books. There are a variety of methods of presenting tatting instructions, but I will use the following style consistently, explaining other styles in brief in a later lesson.

Functionally picots are small loops of material that add interest to a motif. Crocheted, knitted, and bobbin laces, and macramé all use picots to elaborate designs. They use them less often than tatting does for joining one motif to another.

Tatting makes a specialty, even a major focus, of the picot. It's probably the single most important structure beyond the double stitch, because it allows the artist to join various aspects of a design to one another. Petals of flowers can be joined by picots, as also series of daisies to one another, and chains to flowers and other structures:

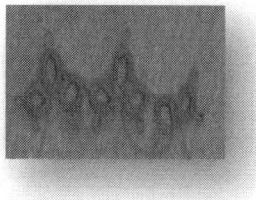  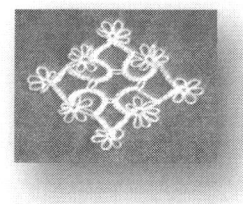

Picots Used as Joins and as Decorative Motifs

Picots can even make a chain into a type of ring:

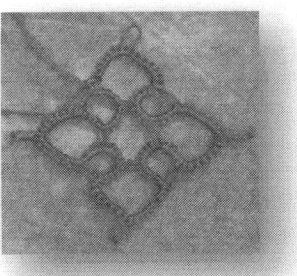

Chain Joined by Picots into a Ringed Structure

They also join motifs into larger items like table clothes, bedspreads, place mats, necklaces and doilies by joining picots between them:

Picots Joining Motifs

Similarly they can join motifs into three dimensional objects like Christmas balls and bells:

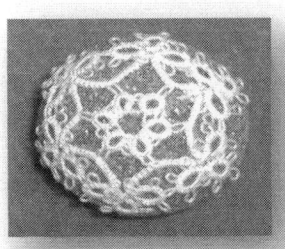 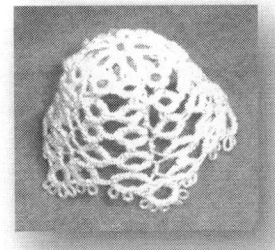

Three Dimensional Objects Depending upon Picots for Structure

Mechanically speaking a picot is simply a section of thread left between two double stitches to create a small gap. Rather than pushing the first half of a double stitch in progress against the previous double stitch, the tatter anchors it a short distance away from it. Then the second half is made close to the first half as usual. This leaves a small gap between the finished double stitch and its predecessor. Examine the photo below. There is an overhand knot at the far left, followed by three completed double stitches, then a length of thread creating a gap, followed by a completed double stitch.

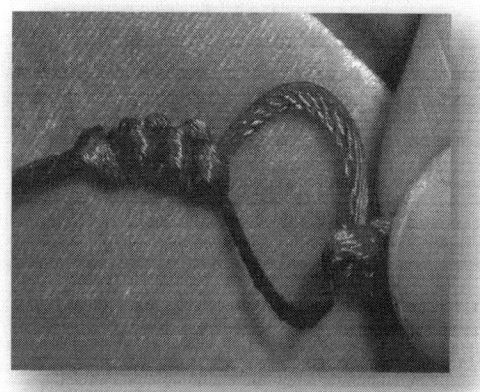

Gap of Thread between Two Successive Double Stitches

When the second double stitch is completed and moved close to its predecessor, the length of ball thread (light in the photograph) that covered the gap rises above the two, forming an arc called a picot, while the shuttle thread (black in the

Finished Picot above Two Successive Double Stitches

photograph) slides through the double stitches to move them closer together.
  Note that it is here that the difference between a knot and a true double

stitch is apparent even in chains and even in those using the same color thread, since *a knot will not slide*.

This is also where a "gap" is not only acceptable it's an expected and planned part of the design. While unintended gaps can give a row of double stitches a messy appearance, an intended well formed picot will add to the design.

Below is a tatted medallion of double stitches in chains and rings with picots used as decorative aspects of both and as connecting bridges between the rings and with the pearls:

Picots in a Medallion Design

Some patterns require different sizes of picot, usually labeling them "small picot" and "large picot" or simply "sp" and "lp" in the instructions. Often where this is the case, the pattern will state the approximate size of both, i.e.) $1/8^{th}$ inch and $1/4^{th}$ inch. The exact size is often a matter of what looks best to the tatter and requires a degree of experience, especially with different sizes of thread.

A gradation in the sizes of picots can help create different effects, and a large number of closely spaced picots tend to have a light and lacy or feathery look depending upon the thread used. While this can be very beautiful, the caveat is that they are also laborious to keep up, especially in finer threads, since they have a tendency to twist when washed and need to be pinned out during drying to keep them looking well. The more of them there are, the more work they will be to keep them looking nice. If, however, you plan on gluing the motif to a card, or covering the surface with a medium to keep it clean, or using glue or starch to fix the pattern more permanently, this aspect of the picot may be less of an issue.

As you might have guessed, the picot is also something to be mastered by way of technique. Try to make them as uniform as possible throughout your pattern. Here too, *control* is what is at issue for the student.

In working a pattern it is especially important to note that picots are only counted as "number of picots" in a pattern; they are not a "stitch" as such. Furthermore, the double stitches which help create them are counted as part of the double stitches in the pattern and not separately as "picot" double stitches. If the pattern calls for "five double stitches, five picots separated by two double stitches, and five double stitches," the pattern will have a total of 18 double stitches. The first double stitch of the first picot is the last of the previous five double stitches. There is no "picot double stitch." The picot is just a "gap," and the number of picots is simply indicating how many times this gap should appear. The number of double stitches merely indicates how many should be before, between and after each gap.[10]

A tatting pattern usually indicates, with various abbreviations and in appropriate sections, what the tatter should do to complete a section of a design. Some patterns, as the one below, consist of a single section; others may have several sections for a single motif, and possibly several motifs to a single project. Here the design is simply a short chain, like the one in Lesson 3, with the addition of picots for interest and practice.

In reading this pattern, the student will see that there are 10 double stitches (ds), then 1 picot (p), which pattern is repeated the number of times necessary to fit the wrist, then ended by 10 double stitches. If the design had required a set number of repeats, this would have been indicated either in written instructions as below, or as a number inside brackets, i.e. [twice] or [four times]. If your bracelet had required 6 picots as it did in mine, the instructions would have said "*10ds, 1p* [six times], 10 ds" or "repeat between ** six times" etc. This same form of instruction is often used in knitting and crocheting as well so should be recognized by anyone already familiar with those crafts.

Work the pattern below as indicated to make your project.

Pattern:

10 ds, 1 p as indicated, 10ds. (That is, 10 double stitches and a picot as many times as needed, then 10 ds). Tie the ends after the last ds, and cut free from the shuttle and ball threads leaving a length of thread for finishing as below.

---

[10] The reason I belabor this point is that it took me years before I figured this out, with the result that some of my earlier work was a little lopsided due to my inaccurate count.

Finishing:
Add a pendant or some other type of focal to the chain if desired, using a head- or eye-pin and jump-ring if needed. Add a clasp to either end of the chain, or tie the ends together. If the latter, glue the knot with craft glue and cut the remaining ends. Cover the knot with a crimp cover.

> *In creating a picot the difference between a knot and a true double stitch is apparent, even in chains, since a knot will not slide to close it.*

Lesson 4: Joining Chains for Elaboration

Project: Necklace of two or more chains joined (j) to one another through picots.

Three Chain Necklace with Died Shell Embellishments

Purpose: Learn to join (j) chains to one another by the means of picots
Continue to practice the double stitch (ds) and picot (p)
Practice reading a pattern

Materials: Crochet cotton or other thread in desired color(s), (the illustration is in black crochet cotton for both ball and shuttle threads, but two colors can be used if needed).
Tatting shuttle
Tape measure
Pendant or other ornament(s) if desired (see below for illustration)
Jewelry findings if needed: clasp, crimp pin cover, head- or eye-pins, jump-rings, etc. as needed
Glue adhesive
Scissors

Length: As desired, (here 9 inches, with silk mouse tail added to tie at desired level around the neck).

Discussion:

At this point you will probably feel confident enough to dispense with a second color of thread for your chains, but don't be discouraged if you still need this cue to prevent knots. It's better to avoid the frustration of starting over or removing the knots while your hands are learning the technique. When you feel able to do your work in one color, give it a try.[11] As illustrated, this project is in one color thread, but it does not have to be worked this way. One might start with one color for the ball thread and another for the shuttle, and then make the second row of chains the reverse. Be sure to select for the ball thread, the color you want to show in your chain.

Picots are the design element that gives tatting its versatility. In this lesson, you will learn to use the picot to join a second chain to a first. Like the bracelet, this project begins with a chain of double stitches and picots of a desired length, but it differs in that the second row is a chain with alternating picots and joins.

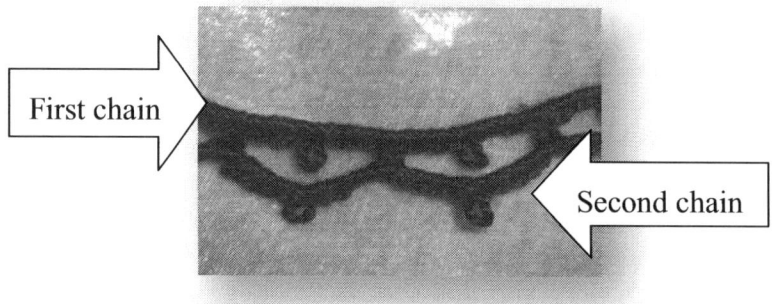

Two Chains with Picots and Joins

A *join* is actually a double stitch which captures a picot between its two halves. It is the method by which two design elements are connected. Essentially, the ball thread of the working chain (here the lower one) is pulled up through a picot in a previously made chain (above in the photo) to create a loop (next photo).[12]

---

[11] Note that the use of two threads will also permit you to experiment with threads of two different sizes and to use a shuttle thread of one fiber to "bulk up" a ball thread that is too thin to produce a desired size of product on its own. A thin metallic thread over a larger cotton thread is an example. Note here, however, that it will require more double stitches to cover the larger thread and to achieve a desired length.

[12] There are other uses for this procedure which will be described and explained later in lesson 9.

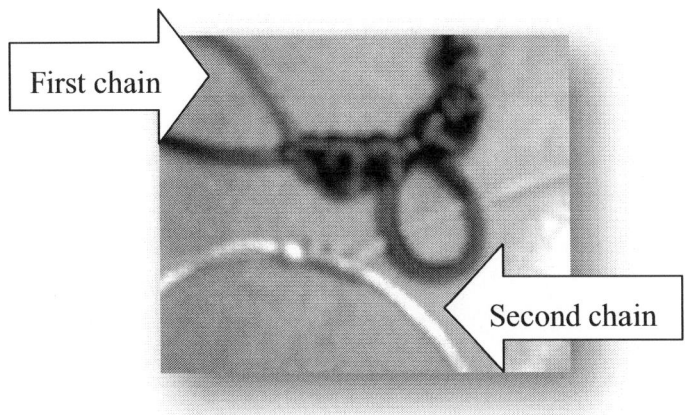

Ball Thread (white) beneath Picot (black) of a Previous Chain

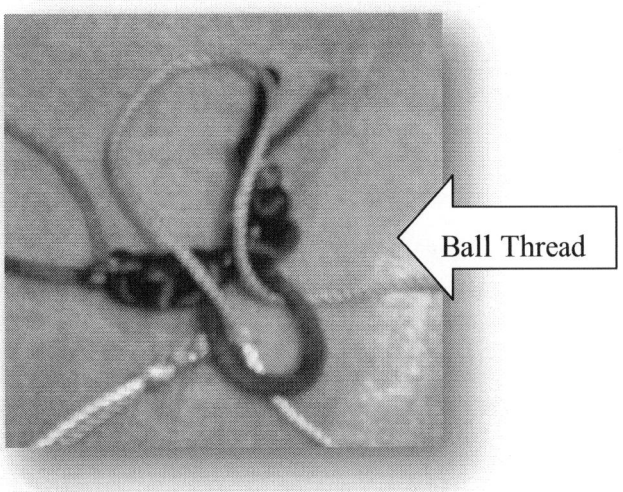

Looping the Ball Thread through the Picot to Start a Join

The shuttle then passes from below and through the loop, as it would for the first half of a normal double stitch. Here too, the shuttle thread is pulled into a taught line.

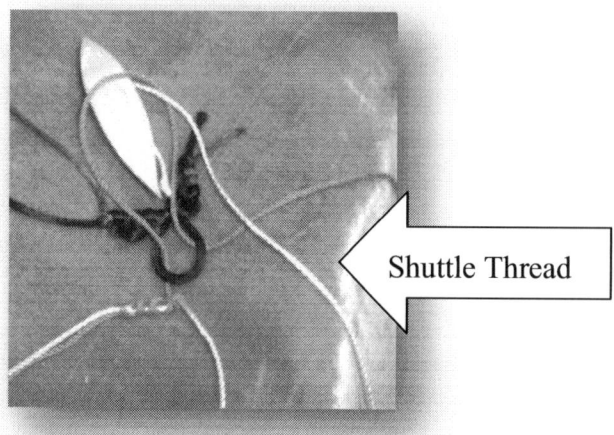

Passing the Shuttle through the Loop

This allows the ball thread to form a loop over it and inside the picot of the first chain. Having completed the first half of the double stitch join, the second half of the double stitch is then completed as usual.

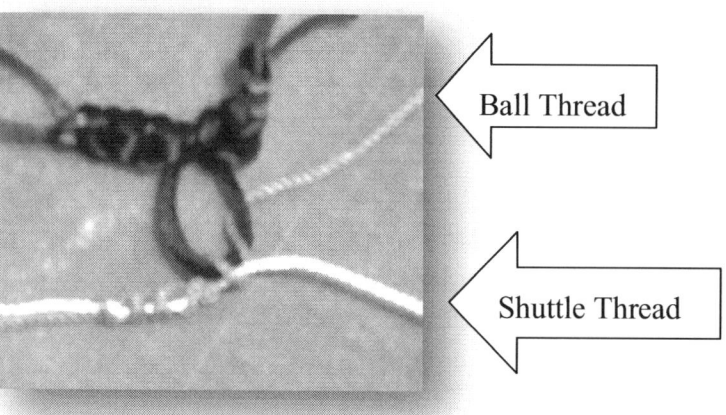

The First Half of the Join

This effectively connects the two chains by entrapping the ball thread of the second chain inside the picot of the previously made chain before continuing with the design.

Second Half of the Double Stitch to Complete the Join

The rest of the pattern is completed as written and as though the first chain did not exist until it is required for the next join scheduled by the pattern. This probably sounds terribly complicated, but in actual practice it is fairly clear once the technique of the join itself is understood.

Any number of chains can be connected in this manner to craft a more elaborate pattern. The method is the same irrespective of the actual number of chains joined.

Study the photo below by way of illustration:

Chain Connected to the Previous Chains with Picots and Joins

As can be seen here, a third row of chain, this one with five picots, is joined to the previous chain at intervals, producing an even more elaborate design. One might even add another row by joining a chain in the center picot of each of the motifs in this one. It is, in fact, in this way that very elaborate lace collars are created for blouses or sweaters. Some very fine examples of this type of collar appear in *The*

Tatters Treasure Chest.[13]

Pattern:

<u>Row One</u>: Tie ball and shuttle threads together. Chain *5 ds,1 p.* Repeat pattern between the stars until desired length is obtained, ending with an odd number of picots, then 5 ds. Tie the ends after the last ds, and cut free from the shuttle and ball threads leaving a length of thread for finishing.

<u>Row Two</u>: Tie ball and shuttle threads together. Pull the ball thread up into a loop through the first picot of the first chain, then pass the shuttle up from below and through the loop. Gently tighten both threads until the picot is against the starting knot. Perform the second half of a double stitch (shuttle down from above) [join completed].[14] *5 ds,[15] 1 p, 5ds, j to the next odd numbered picot (that is, skip one picot, then join to the next)* repeat the pattern between the stars until the final join with the previous chain, then cut from the shuttle and ball threads and tie off, leaving a length of thread for finishing.

Necklace of Two Rows, Second Chain Connected to the First with Picots and Joins

Note that it is perfectly legal to finish off the necklace at this point if you prefer it that way. You might add pendants of some type to the picots—lower or upper ones—or the joins with head- or eye-pins if you wish, or you could weave a

---

[13] *The Tatter's Treasure Chest*, Mary Carolyn Waldrep, Dover Publications, 1990.
[14] Note that a join is a double stitch around the joining picot. It is not finished until the second half of the double stitch is completed.
[15] Remember that the join is itself a double stitch and counts as one of the five here.

ribbon through the spaces created between the two chains by the joining picots. If you prefer something more elaborate or to practice the join further, continue on to row three.

Row Three: Tie ball and shuttle threads together. Pull the ball thread up into a loop through the first picot of the first chain, then pass the shuttle thread up from below and through the loop. Gently tighten both threads until the join is against the starting knot. Perform the second half of the ds (shuttle down from above) [join completed]. * 5 ds, 5 p separated by 2ds, 5ds, j to next p in the previous chain* repeat until the last join, then tie and cut from the ball and shuttle threads leaving a length of thread for finishing.

Third Row 5 Picot Chain Connected to the Previous Chains with Picots and Joins

Finishing: Glue each knot and tie-off in chains two and three, then cut as close to the knots as possible. Use ribbon, satin cord, chain or other type of material attached to the remaining thread of the first chain for ties to fasten the finished necklace at whatever length is desired; alternately, add clasps to the first chain. Leave the lace as it is or add embellishments of some kind, joining these to picots or joins as desired with head- or eye-pins.

As mentioned before, any number of additional rows could be added by the same method. Similarly, a variety of picot patterns might also be used to increase or decrease the elaboration of each successive chain, creating differences in the shapes of the spaces between them.

The design, with or without embellishments might be sewn to the neck opening of a sweater or blouse. Similarly, a pair of identical designs might be sewn to form the left and right half of a decorative collar around the opening of either.

Below are examples of different treatments of the same tatted necklace of three rows. In this instance the embellishments would be added after the fact with head- or eye-pins or jump-rings. This allows a variety of treatments to be tested without a commitment until a desired effect is obtained. In one of the following lessons beads will be added to the design from the beginning using the ball thread to secure them in place.

Variations on a Theme of Chains

Lesson 5: The chain as motif—the "reverse work" instruction

Project: Square or diamond chain motif

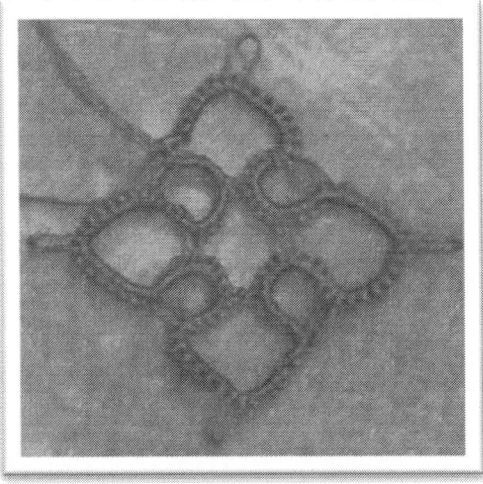

Purpose: Learn the "reverse work" instruction
Continue to practice the double stitch (ds) and picot (p)
Practice reading a pattern

Discussion:

As can be seen in Lesson 4, the simple chain need hardly be deemed the poor relation of the ring. In fact, it can be used for very elaborate designs. Though it can also form an individual motif, and thereby larger projects, the basic chain with picots when worked this way can become rather confusing especially for the beginner. Essentially a chain is worked with picots placed at specific points. Further extensions of the chain are then joined to these picots in an order which fixes them in place and creates a finished motif. While there are not many such designs out there, some very interesting examples exist. The so-called "Celtic" tatting uses this method almost exclusively and with the best results I've ever seen.[16]

---

[16] I refer the student to *Celtic Tatting, Knots and Patterns* by Rozella F. Linden, listed in the bibliography, for a wonderful collection of these motifs.

The instruction most often used to turn the chain onto itself, as for instance with the above square motif, is "reverse work" or RW.[17] As the work is in progress whenever a sharp distinction in the direction of the stitches is required, the entire chain is reversed so that the next double stitches made are facing in the opposite direction of those made before them. There is no actual difference in how the stitches are made, no other device that keeps the new stitches in the new direction. Because the thread tends to "remember" the positions of the various stitches—probably as a result of areas of stretch and the absence of it—an interruption of the work occurs which becomes part of the design.

Take note at this point, that these chain designs can be very confusing, both as written works and in the actual process of tatting them. If you wish to delay this lesson until you feel more comfortable with the process of tatting itself, you may continue on to the next lesson without suffering a lack of a technique for having done so. Reverse work will be discussed again in a later lesson, and the pattern itself will be used again in Lesson 13. It is included here primarily because it is another use for the chain with picots, and because it helps to explain the process and uses of the reverse work instruction.

For those who wish to attempt this use of chains, I include the following pattern and illustrations.

Pattern:

Square or Diamond Chain Motif:

Study the following illustrations for guidance. Tie the shuttle & ball threads together. Note that all picots should be generous. It will help to keep all double stitches on the corners (the 8ds) loose and those in the loops (the 5ds) tighter. Doing so will cause a curl which will make the design clearer and the working process more apparent.

Start the chain beginning with a p, using the knot of the ball and shuttle threads as the first "ds" forming it, then 8ds [remembering that the second ds for the p counts as the 1st of the 8], p, 8ds, p, [1st corner

---

[17] Reverse work as described here is a verb of command, not a noun. Reverse work as a descriptive noun is a technique that produces double stitches along the opposite thread on a ring in process; it creates the visual effect of two halves rather than a continuous ring. Here it is a technique to create a pronounced change of direction in a chain. See also below, Lesson 9, where it is used to make the chains on either side of a single ring appear more continuous.

made].

Reverse work (RW), 5ds, p, 5ds, p, 5ds [1st interior loop made].
RW, j to the 3rd p[18] from the beginning [which joins 2nd corner to the 1st], 8ds, p, 8ds, p [2nd corner made].

RW, 5ds, j to 4th free p from beg [the second p on the 1st loop], 5ds, p, 5ds [2nd interior loop made].

RW, j to 5th free p [the last p made on the 2nd corner] from beg [joins 3rd corner to 2nd], 8ds, p, 8ds, p [3rd corner made].

RW, 5 ds, j to second p on the 2nd loop, 5ds, p, 5ds [3rd interior loop].

RW, j to last p made on the 3rd corner [joins the 4th corner to the 3rd], 8 ds, p, 8 ds [4th corner made], j to first picot of the first corner [closing the motif at the corners].

RW, 5 ds, j to last free p of previous (3rd) interior loop, 5ds, j to the remaining free picot of the 1st interior loop, 5 ds, cut and tie thread into to starting threads of the chain [completing the 4th interior loop].[19]

Because this type of tatted work can appear very convoluted as it is worked—it looks a little snaky in progress—it is useful to think of it as an edging for the first three corners and their associated loops. The final corner and its finishing loop bring the edging around to the beginning, completing the motif. Examine the following labeled photos to see the process as it unfolds.

---

[18] If you have followed the suggestions at the beginning of the instructions, the joining picot should be readily apparent at each point a join is required.

[19] It is here more than anywhere else where schematic tatting instructions are the most useful, and it is also here that they are most often found. See Lesson 15 for further information on alternative tatting instruction.

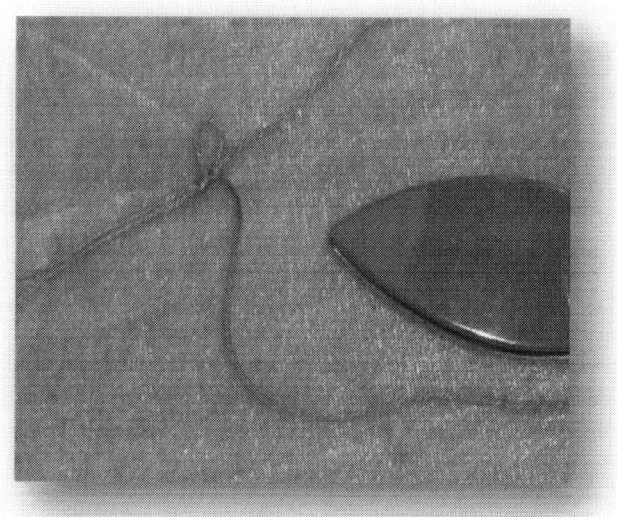

First Picot with Tie Knot as First Double Stitch

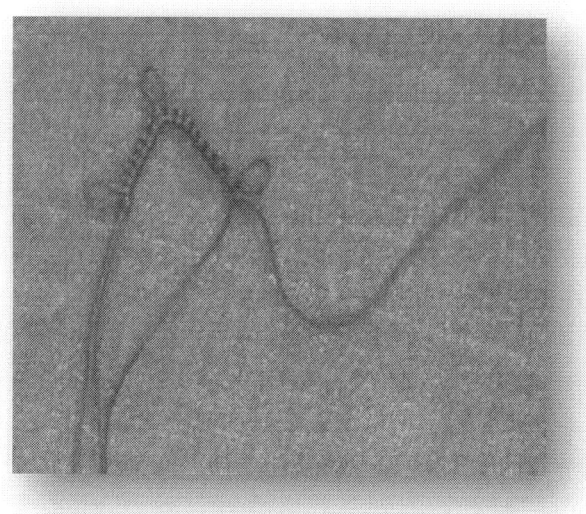

First Corner before the Reverse Work

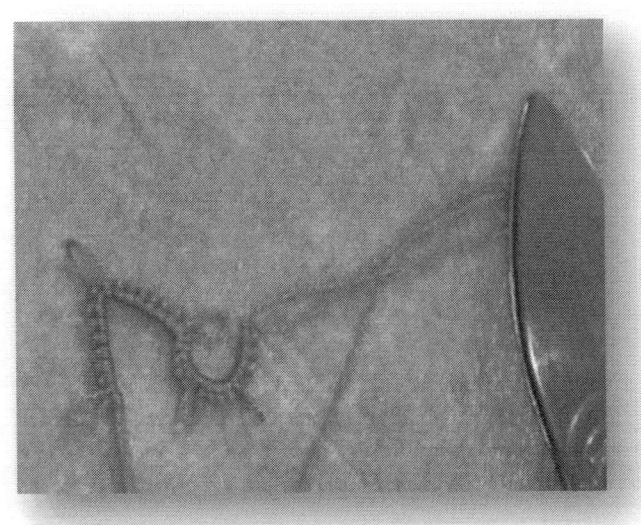

Reverse Work of First Loop

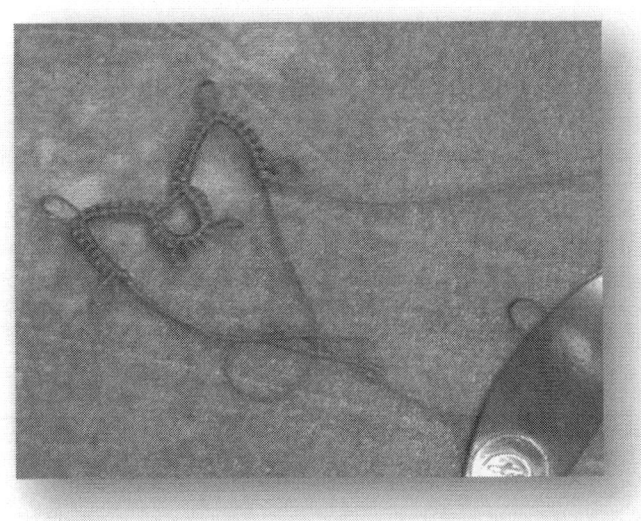

Join for First Loop and Second Corner

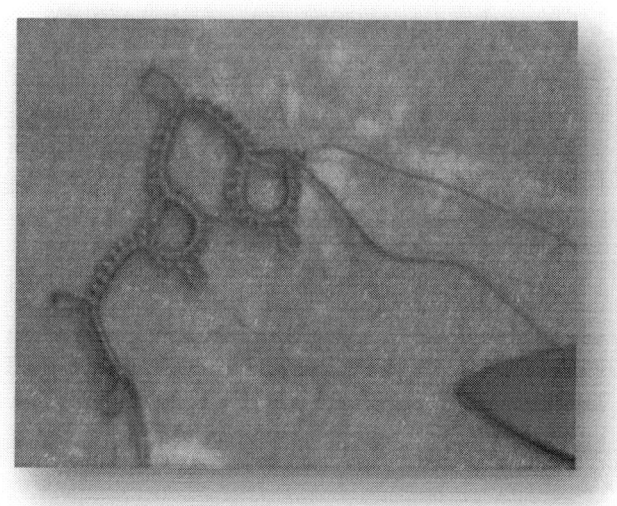

Second Loop and Join

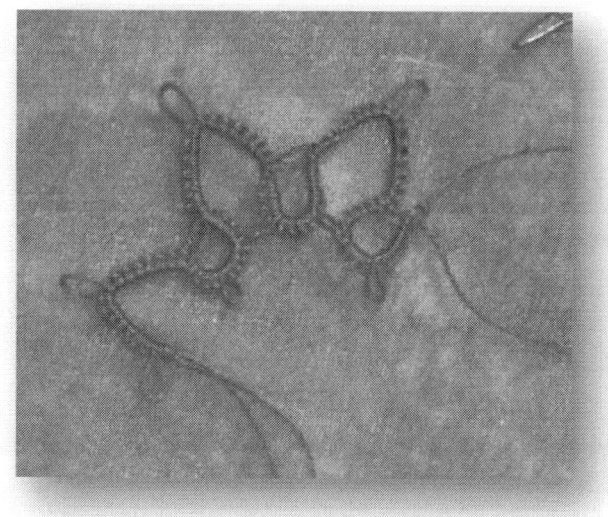

Third Corner and Loop with Joins

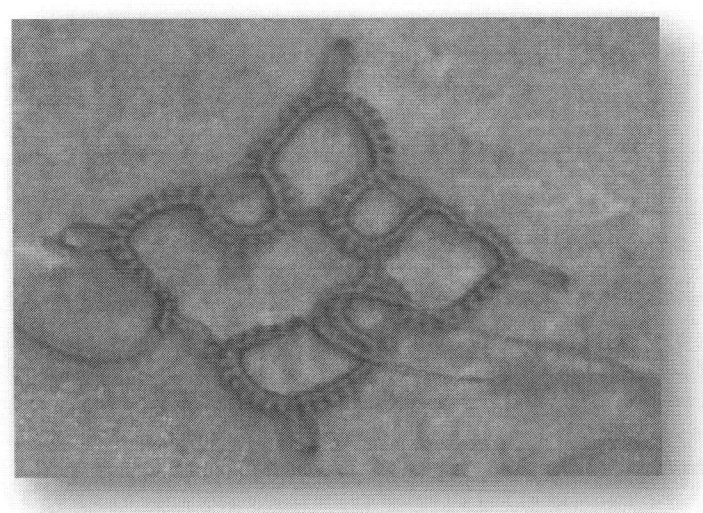

Forth Corner Joined to First

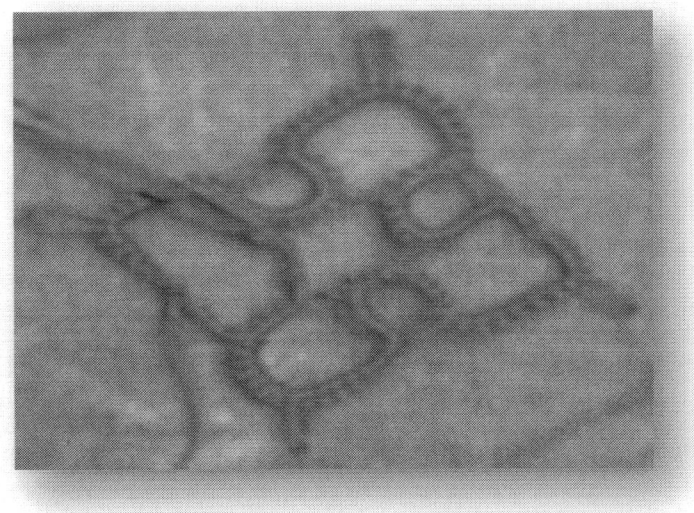

Picot of the First Motif and Second Join of the Fourth Loop

Final Join to the First Corner and Finished Motif

The student will readily appreciate the importance of the introductory instructions accompanying the pattern. By keeping the corner stitches (the 8ds) loose and the loop stitches the 5ds) tight, the design takes form more naturally, readily revealing the proper joining picot at each stage of the working process which ensures that the motif itself has the desired form when finished.

As can be seen from the last photo, the free picots of this motif provide a means for varying the use of the design. Adding beads, crystals, pearls or other items to the free picots will produce an appliqué or jewelry piece. By using them for joins with similar motifs, they would also allow the basic design to be enlarged to any size desired, from doily to bedspread. Examples of the latter will be discussed in Lesson 15.

Notice how this motif differs from one using rings as well as chains:

Motif using Rings as Well as Chains

By the simple expedient of adding rings, the chains have assumed a crisper character, while the picots on the rings add a more floral spirit.

Lesson 6: Adding beads to your tatting

Project: **Bracelet of double stitches and beads**

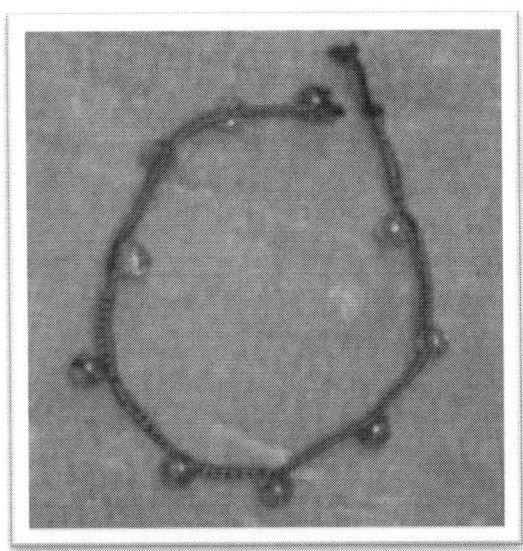

Bracelet of Double Stitches and Beads

Purpose: Learn to add beads to a tatted design
Continue to practice the double stitch (ds) and picot (p)
Practice reading a pattern

Materials: Crochet cotton or other thread in desired color(s) (here purple nylon line and black crochet cotton)
Tatting shuttle
Jewelry needle
20 pearls, beads, or other ornament(s) (here 6 mm glass beads)
Tape measure
Clasp if desired or crimp cover
Glue adhesive
Scissors
Jewelry pliers

Length: Large enough to fit the wrist if clasps are used or over the widest part of the hand with the thumb folded inward if knotted.

Discussion:

You can add interest to your tatted works by adding beads to them. This is where lace and jewelry cross paths with very productive results. It is also where even the beginner can start to become a creative designer. Since design is essentially the selection among alternate choices at different points in the creation of an art work and everyone makes choices every day, everyone also has the capacity to design.

With tatting it starts with the first choice of the type and color of thread you'll use. One can easily break away from a published pattern simply by changing the color or the material of the thread used. In this lesson the addition of beads provides a new twist on the old pattern of chain, double stitches and picots presented in previous lessons.

With beads, there are three possible--probably more--methods of attaching them to tatted work. One can add them to a finished work with sewing thread or glue; the sewer might prefer this. Alternately one may add them with jewelry chain links or eye pins. Anyone familiar with jewelry making might prefer this method. We looked at these methods in previous lessons. In this case, the student will learn to add them to the ball thread and position them as he or she works the pattern.

Placing beads in the process of tatted work is something which requires a degree of planning, since the number of beads required must be known at least in general and that number threaded onto the ball thread[20] before beginning the project. In the illustration for this lesson, a bracelet about the circumference of the wrist, some 20 beads should be more than sufficient. Any unneeded beads can be removed when cutting the completed project from the ball and shuttle threads during the finishing process. Even with longer works a "guesstimation" may be fully adequate.

While this project uses a single color of bead, some projects may require two or more colors in patterns. In such a case the beads need to be strung in the color groups that will be needed during the tatting process. For instance if a triad of beads in two colors appears in the design with two of one color flanking one in a second color, the beads will have to be strung along the ball thread in the order

---

[20] There are also instances when the beads would be threaded onto the shuttle thread before it is wound onto the shuttle itself, see below Lesson 11.

in which they must appear in the project, so that they are ready to be placed in position as your design progresses. Note that beads may be placed singly or in groups on individual picots. The former creates a more linear look, while the latter creates clusters.

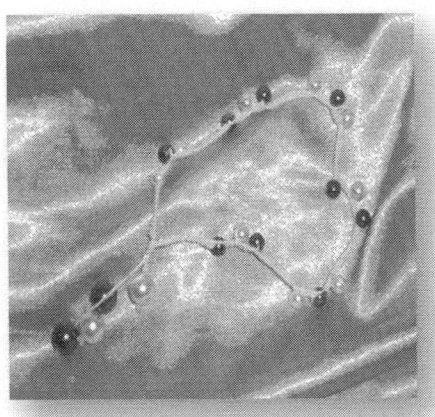 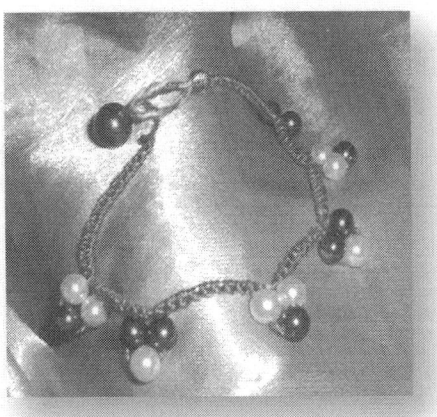

Bead Patterns in Different Colors
Left as Individual Beads on Separate Picots and Right as Bead Clusters on Single Picots

The stringing of beads onto the ball thread requires a long narrow jewelry needle. This special needle has a lengthy, collapsible eye comprising almost the entire length of the needle. The eye can be opened to admit almost any thread

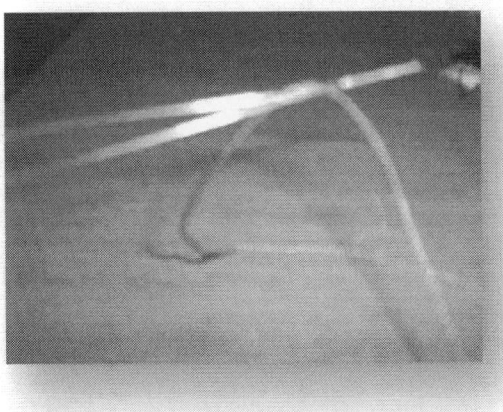

Beading Needle

size then allowed to collapse for use. Because the eye is very flat, it passes through the opening in beads much more easily than a standard sewing needle can.

By adding the required number of beads to the ball thread and sliding them out of the way during regular tatting and sliding them into place as needed, the thread becomes a repository of available beads. Even without knowing the exact number of beads that will be needed in the finished project, the tatter can prepare by threading enough and "then some," since the beads will be out of the way until needed.

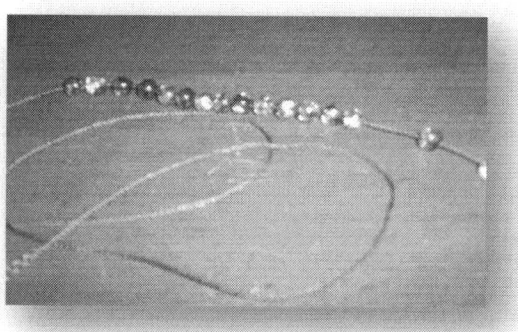

Beads Threaded on the Ball Thread for Tatting

Adding beads to a work in progress is much like adding picots. Essentially the bead uses the picot thread as the method of placement.[21] The appropriate number of double stitches are first placed as the pattern directs, then instead of creating a picot, a bead or beads is/are moved into the space between the flanking double stitches along the length of thread that would have been a picot had it remained empty. Make certain that the next double stitch is as close as possible to that preceding the bead so that the shuttle thread does not show through on either side of the bead.[22]

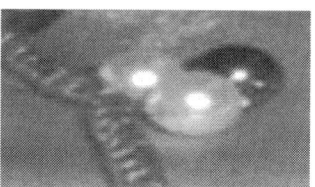

Beads Placed on a Picot with Thread Drawn Closely beneath Them

---

[21] Actually the beads may also be placed on the base or shuttle thread as well, though this is less often done. See Lesson 12, beginning page 89.

[22] This may not be possible in all cases, especially with a coarser thread. In the illustrated project, the less bulky ball thread manages to get beneath the bead fairly well, though not always.

Pattern:

Insert the tail of the ball thread into a jewelry needle and proceed to thread 15-20 beads onto it, sliding them over and out of the way of the needle.

Remove the needle, and if a bead and loop closure is desired, tie one bead onto a loop of the end of the ball thread, then tie the ball and shuttle threads together just after it.

Chain of *10 ds, 1 bead.* Repeat the pattern between the stars until the bracelet is the desired length, ending with 10 ds. Tie off and cut the work from the ball and shuttle threads, leaving a length of thread for finishing. You will be removing the unused beads in the process.

Finishing:

Make an overhand knot to create a loop of thread on the end that does not have a bead. Glue and cut the remaining threads as close as possible. Use the thread loop to catch the bead at the other end as a closure.

Alternately, leave the threads long, add beads to each of the ends and pass these through the loop.

Alternately, add a jewelry clasp to both ends to close, or tie the end threads together, glue and cut them, then cover the knot with a crimp cap.[23]

For Additional practice make a bracelet using the instructions above, except move two or three beads into the space, forming clusters of beads. Finish as before.

---

[23] Remember that your type of closure will depend upon whether you chose to end your bracelet at wrist width or at hand width.

Placing beads in the process of tatted work is something which requires a degree of planning, since the number of beads required must be known at least in general and that number threaded onto the ball thread before beginning the project.

PART TWO: Rings

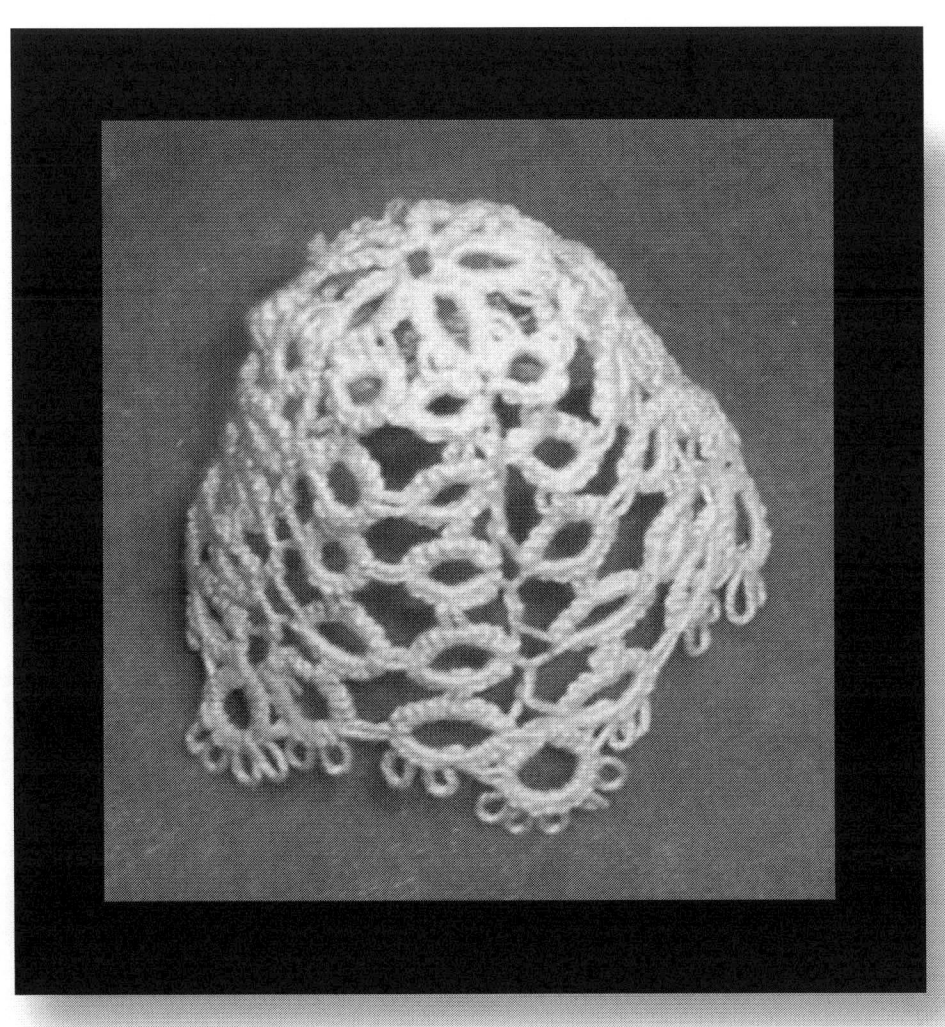

Lesson 7: Rings—breaking away from the "signals"

Project: Single rings for an edging (kitchen towel)

Kitchen Towel with Single Ring Edging

Purpose: Learn to make rings
Practice the double stitch (ds) and picot (p) on the shuttle thread
Practice reading a pattern
Materials: Crochet cotton or other thread in desired color
Tatting shuttle
Tape measure
Length: As long as needed to edge your project (towels, pillow

case, blouse collar, sleeve edges, handkerchief, note paper, etc.)

Discussion:

For most people tatted *rings* are the gold standard of tatted lace. This is hardly a surprise, since they are cleverly made and serve any number of purposes. A tatted work entirely of chains is impressive, but the addition of rings can create an absolute masterpiece. Furthermore and paradoxically, tatted lace of rings and chains can be produced with far less effort than knitted or crocheted lace. At least it can if you know how to do it! It is little wonder, then, that everyone wants to jump right in with rings at the beginning of their learning, and also little surprise that they nearly always fail in their first attempts, can't understand why, and often give up their efforts in frustration. It is probably for this reason and this alone that tatting is rapidly becoming a "lost art."

Tatted rings are double stitches and picots made with a shuttle thread over the same shuttle thread wrapped around the left hand, starting and ending between the thumb and index finger. Because of this, properly made double stitches can be slipped together into a closed circle by pulling the thread through them, removing the extra base thread. Any knots that the tatter may have introduced by mistake are usually unnoticed until the effort to close the ring results in failure to close or a break in the thread. There are no "signals" in rings until you've already made the mistakes. Because of this, it is almost always best to begin the actual learning process with chains. When proper double stitches have been learned and their shape and behavior have become readily identifiable by visual inspection, the beginning tatter can progress to rings because he or she will more easily spot a wrong stitch before several have been made.

To begin with, double stitches and picots are made in essentially the same way for rings as they are for chains. The technique and the use of the hands and shuttle are entirely the same. The only difference is that it is the shuttle thread itself that does everything. As can be seen in the next photo, the shuttle thread is wrapped entirely around the fingers of the left hand, and both the tail and the shuttle ends of the thread are stabilized by the thumb and index finger. Because there is no wrapped thread on the little finger, the thread is a complete circle around the fingers; it's not an open arc beginning with the thumb and index finger and ending with the little finger.

Position of the Thread and Fingers for the Ring

    Again as before, to make the first half of a double stitch a loop of the shuttle thread is arranged up and over the thread on the fingers, and the shuttle itself passes up from below and between the loop of thread and the thread around the fingers. The left hand thread is taught (see above), making it appear as a line, which makes it easily identifiable.

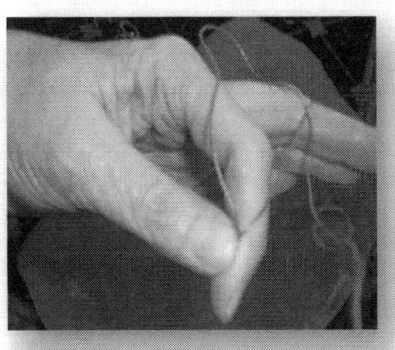 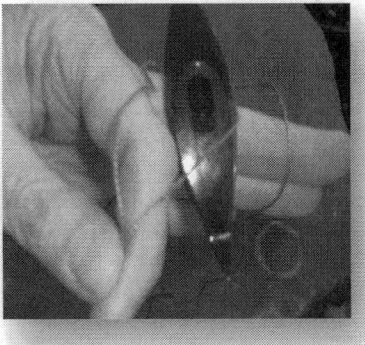

Thread and Shuttle Positions for the First Half of the Double Stitch in a Ring

It is *beneath* this thread the shuttle must pass. Once that pass has been made, a relaxing of the left hand fingers and a simple pull on the shuttle thread to tighten it will start the familiar process of looping which the tatter will recognize as the first half of the double stitch. Here again it will happen almost without effort as long as the shuttle thread is pulled tightly and the fingers of the left hand are used to vary the tension in the working thread around them.

Using the Fingers of the Left Hand to Position the First Half of the Double Stitch in a Ring

The second half of the double stitch is made in the same way as with chains. A loop of shuttle thread is dropped down and across the finger thread and the shuttle is passed down from above between the two threads. The shuttle is then pulled away from the work allowing the left hand to form a loop and close the two halves of the double stitch. Repeating the double stitch will produce a phalanx of them around the circle of the working thread.

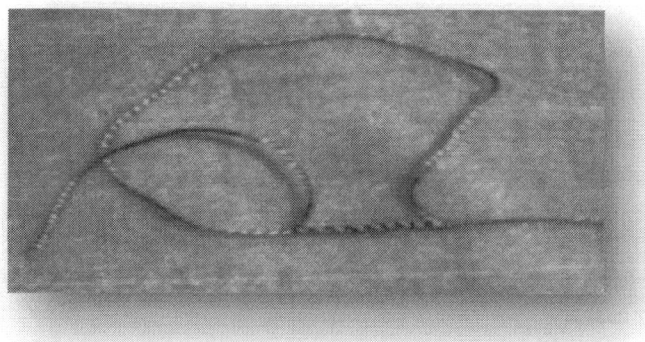

Series of Double Stitches on a Ring

Picots are also added in the manner of a chain. A double stitch is followed by a space and a second double stitch is made. When the second has been finished, the gap is closed by sliding the two together along the base thread.

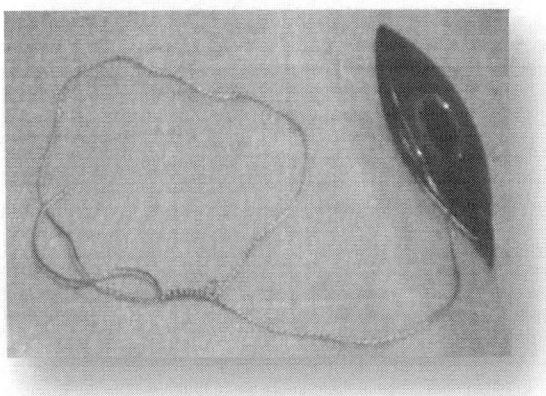

Double Stitches and a Picot on a Ring

By following such a picot with a similar pattern of double stitches after it—or indeed any set of picot and double stitch patterns—the truly unique quality of the ring becomes self-evident. By drawing on the shuttle thread and stabilizing the tatted section of the motif, the work will gradually close into a ring—that famous tatted ring that everyone wants to do.[24]

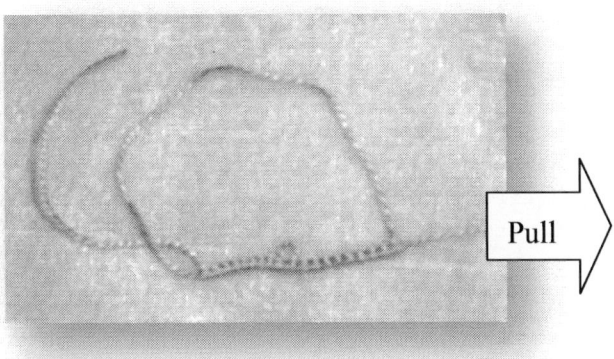

Closing the Ring

---

[24] Note that different types of thread will pull closed with differing degrees of difficulty. Some cotton threads, yarns, and definitely macramé twine will pull closed with more resistance than silk or nylon. If the stitches seem to be tightening when you increase your effort to close the ring, there is probably a knot.

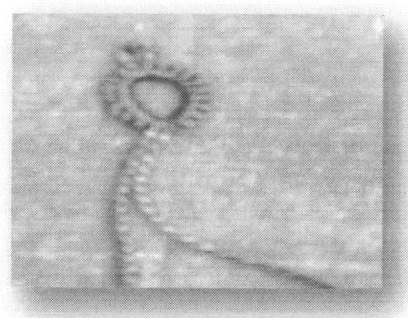

Completed Series of Double Stitches and Picot on a Closed Ring

Pattern:

<u>First ring</u>: Anchoring the tail end of the shuttle thread between the thumb and index finger, wrap the thread around the hand and back to the thumb and index finger. Hold the two ends securely; then drape a loop of the shuttle thread over the thread on the left hand. Pass the shuttle up and between the left hand thread and the loop thread. Pull the shuttle thread tightly and gently encourage the loop appearing in the hand thread to move toward the thumb and index finger. Secure this, the first half of the double stitch, with the thumb and index finger so that it does not escape. Loop the shuttle thread downward over the left hand thread and pass the shuttle down and between the two threads. Pull the shuttle thread tight with the right hand, encouraging a loop to form on the left hand thread, moving it close to the first half of the double stitch. The completed double stitch will now help to secure the ring and act as a "brake" for the next stitches. Notice that these stitches are like those of the chains you made earlier and that they are also made with the same types of movements. The only difference is that you are making them on the same thread with which you're working them.

You may find that your working thread becomes too short and tight to maneuver. If this happens, and it will, release some of the shuttle thread by unwinding it, then loosen the hand thread by pulling it back through the double stitches from the shuttle thread to give you more space and more thread with which to work. This is opposite of the pull to close the ring. By opening and partially closing the ring, you can check the correctness of your stitches. If the thread doesn't move back and forth, you've made knots. If it does, you've made double stitches. By doing this periodically, you will be given ample notice of errors, saving you a lot of frustration.

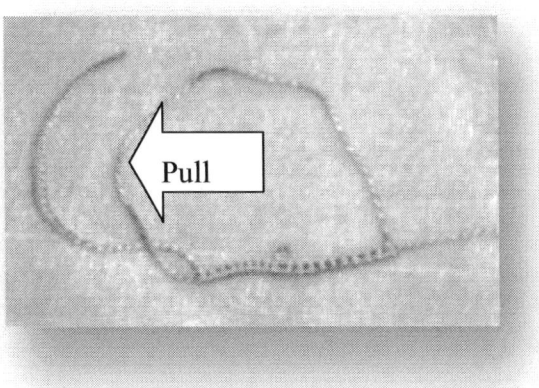

Opening the Ring Thread

Next, perform 4 more ds (bringing the number up to 5), p, 5 ds, p[25], 5 ds, p 5ds. You should now have three picots and a total of 20 double stitches. Now close the ring by pulling the shuttle thread gently through the stitches while holding firmly onto them.

The shuttle thread should move easily through the work and gradually disappear from the circle of thread that surrounded the left hand. If not, check your double stitches to make sure their configuration is the π shape you expect. If there is one that is irregular, undo the stitches with the point of your shuttle or a crochet hook, working back until you have removed the irregular stitch,

---

[25] You can vary our design quite simply by making your picots of different sizes; small ones flanking a large central picot is the most common variation. You could also change the design by adding more picots than called for, especially by making three close together instead of a single central picot as in the pattern.

then redo the pattern from that point and try to close again. First ring made.

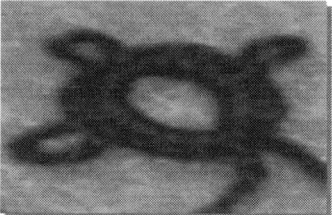

One completed Ring

<u>Second and succeeding rings</u>: Leaving a half inch length of thread between them,[26] start another ring as the first.[27] Repeat until desired length has been achieved.

Finishing: Sew your edging to your project with sewing thread, hiding the spacing threads on the wrong side of the project by anchoring them with small sewn stitches. If the color and character of the spacing thread will add definition to the edge of your project, sew it lightly along the edge rather than behind it with small stitches.

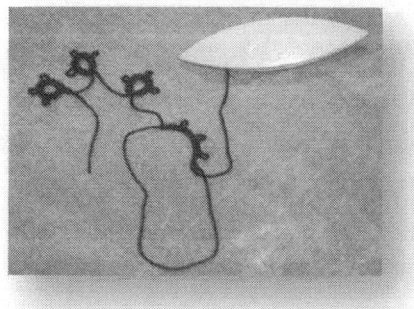

Series of Tatted Rings with Space

---

[26] If you wished, you could join the second ring to the first picot of the first ring after the first 5 ds. This will give you a continuous tape of rings joined by the side picots, leaving only the central picot of each as an "ornament." Here all the picots are ornamental rather than functional. See the next lesson for the joining technique.

[27] You can more equally estimate your spacing thread by measuring the next one against the first and placing your first double stitch as close as possible to the measured distance.

Lesson 8: Joining rings

Project: Rings joined in threes for an edging (holiday hand towel)

Trefoil Pattern on Holiday Towel

Purpose: Learn to join rings
Practice the double stitch (ds) and picot (p) in rings
Practice reading a pattern
Materials: Crochet cotton or other thread in desired color
Tatting shuttle
Tape measure
Length: As long as needed to edge your project (towels, pillow case, blouse collar, sleeve edges, handkerchief, note paper, etc. here a holiday hand towel)

Discussion:

As with chains, the key to elaboration with rings is the picot-join. In this lesson you will join rings with their picots to make a motif and to join these motifs into a continuous edging. In this instance, as in the last lesson, a small spacing thread will separate one motif from its predecessor and will be hidden behind the material of the project to be decorated;

this obviates the need for cutting and tying off each motif as it is finished and speeds the tatting process. The next lesson will focus on the use of chains to eliminate this space and embellish the entire work.

      Imagine if you will, that the rings of the tatted edging below, from the previous lesson, were arranged so that the side picots of each could be "tied" together—which you could certainly do—leaving just the middle picot of each ring free, and you will have the concept of joining rings. The tatter merely substitutes a join for a "tie" while the work is in process, making the edging much neater and more continuous.

Tatted Rings, Separate and Joined

      Joining rings is actually easier to do than joining chains, because often the picot being used is already close to the work in progress; this also makes the process of joining a little more obvious. As in the project above, a ring is completed and a second ring started (photo below). Instead of completing a picot after the first set of double stitches, the base thread—that over which the work is

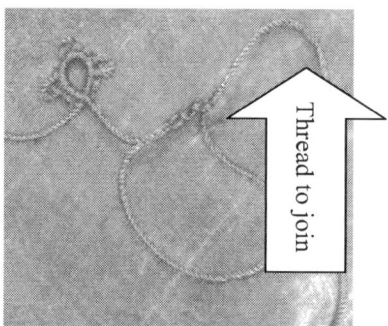

Finished Ring and Started Second

being done—is pulled up through the last picot of the first ring (photo below) and the shuttle passed up from below and through the loop thus made.

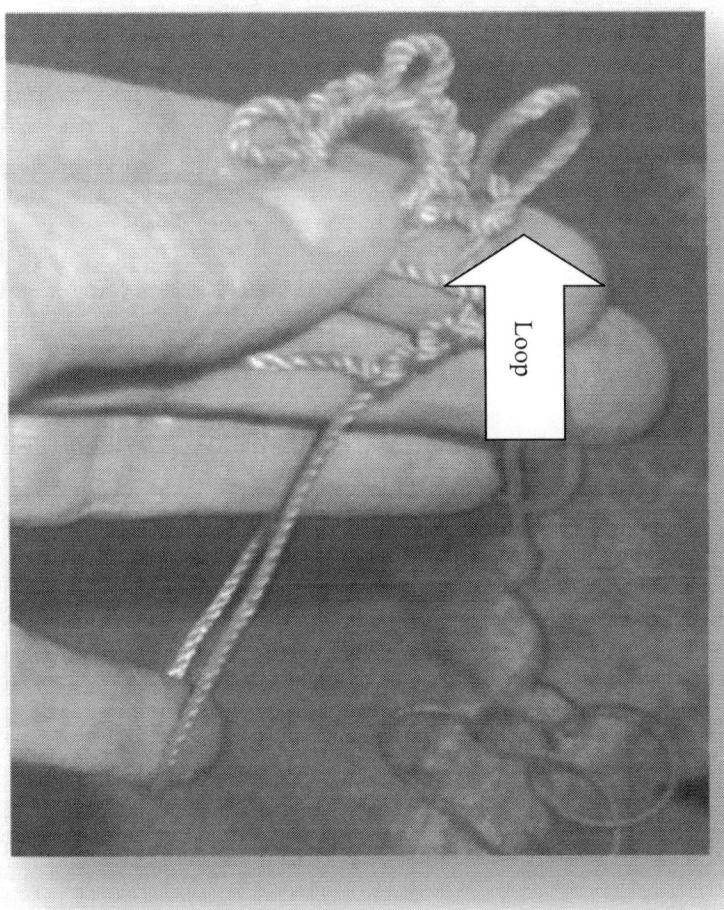

Loop pulled up from Below

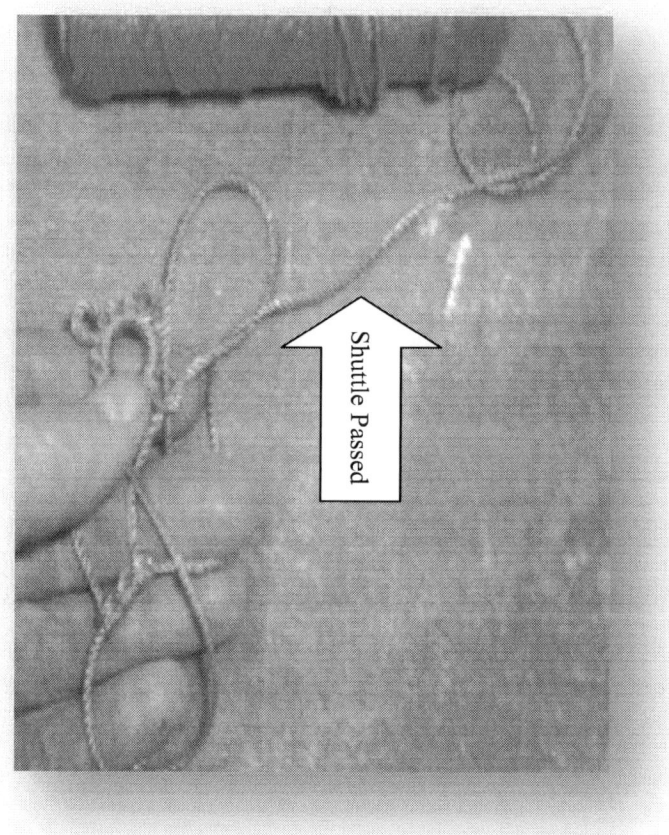

Shuttle Pass from below and Through

Note that to actually perform the maneuver; the base thread around the left hand will have to be slightly enlarged by pulling it back through the double stitches. This widens the circle enough so that it can pass through the picot and still produce a loop large enough above it for the shuttle (here a spool of nylon cord) to pass through it while still keeping everything in control. Care must be taken that the loop does not twist inside the picot, as this will create a knot rather than the desired slip stitch.

This pass of the shuttle completes what is actually the first half of a double stitch inside the picot of the previous ring. Finally the second half of a double stitch is completed as usual (photo below). Thereafter the work is performed as written, and the second ring is closed. Any number of rings can be joined in this manner, creating an edging of the size desired.

First Half Double Stitch/Join

Second Half Double Stitch/Join

Two Closed and Joined Rings

Practice Pattern:

Practice the following pattern to learn joining rings and reading the instructions, then go on to the next for the project.

<u>First Ring</u>.   5 ds, 3 p sep. by 5 ds, 5 ds, cl.
<u>Second Ring</u>.
  Leaving a quarter to a half inch of thread between rings, 5ds, j to last p of last R, 5[28] ds, 2 p separated by 5 ds, 5ds, cl.
Repeat the second ring until the desired length is reached.

If you are still having difficulty with reading patterns with the increasing complexity of the design, this one should be interpreted as:
Five double stitches. Three picots with five double stitches between them and five double stitches after the last one. Close the ring. The next ring follows a length of thread. Perform five double stitches, then pull the thread up through the last picot made in the last ring, pass the shuttle up through the loop made, then perform the last half of the double stitch. Do five double stitches—counting the joining double stitch as one of them—then two picots separated by five double stitches, then five double stitches after the last of these two, then close the ring. All further rings are made like the second.

Having practiced a familiar pattern in a new way, proceed to the lesson pattern. It has only a few minor changes. Here you will be creating a motif and repeating it. You create the motif by merely bringing the bases of the rings close together rather than separating them by lengths of thread. You will also add a single extra double stitch to either side of the middle picot to make the central of the three rings stand out slightly from the two flanking it.

---

[28] Remember that the join is actually counted as one of these double stitches and that you actually need just four more.

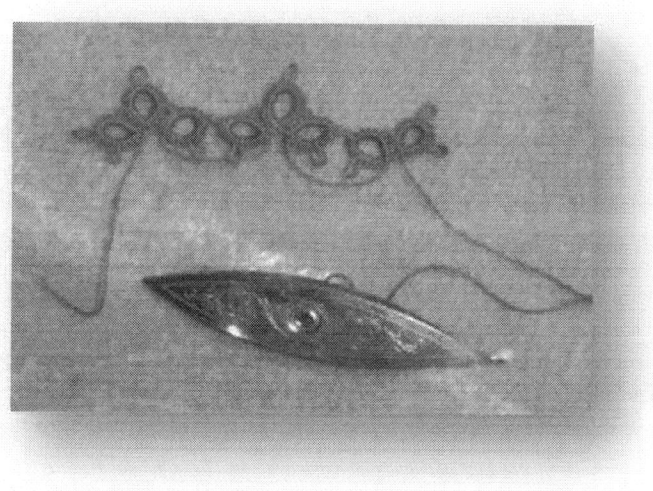

Pattern:

    First Motif:
        First Ring.   5 ds, 3 p sep. by 5 ds, 5 ds, cl.[29]
        Second Ring.
        Starting at the base of the last ring, 5 ds, j to last p of last R, 6 ds, 2 p separated by 6 ds, 5 ds, cl.
        Third Ring. Starting at the base of the last ring, 5 ds, j to last p of last R, 5 ds, 2 p separated by 5 ds, 5ds, cl.
    Second Motif:
        Leave from one to one and a half inch length of thread between the first motif and the first ring of the next.
        First Ring.   5 ds, p, 5ds, j to the 2nd (middle) picot of the last ring of the last motif, 5 ds, p, 5 ds, cl.
        Second Ring. Starting at the base of the last ring, 5 ds, j to last p of last R, 6 ds, 2 p separated by 6 ds, 5ds, cl.
        Third Ring. Starting at the base of the last ring, 5 ds, j to

---

[29] It is important to remember that a ring once closed is virtually impossible to reopen. Better to take a little time to count your picots and double stitches before closure to make certain you have the right number than to close and discover the mistake afterwards. Chains are forgiving; rings almost never are.

last p of last R, 5 ds, 2 p separated by 5 ds, 5ds, cl.
Repeat the second motif until the desired length is reached.

As you work this pattern and compare it to the practice pattern, you can see that a more elaborate motif is created by clustering joined rings in threes. Simple techniques—in fact just decisions[30]—add to a tatted design with very little difficulty and without knowing any more about tatting than already learned by this lesson. This is how many new patterns have been and are created over time.

Note that the open picots on both sides of the motif are pointing down toward the "sewing edge" of the lace border. Although the loops of thread between the motifs can be still be used to attach the lace to the project with small sewn stitches, the picots may also be used for this purpose in like manner.

> *Simple techniques—in fact just decisions—add to a tatted design with very little difficulty and without knowing any more about tatting than already learned by this lesson. This is how many new patterns have been and are created over time.*

---

[30] See appendices below.

Lesson 9: Avoiding the thread spaces

Projects: Rings with chains joining motifs

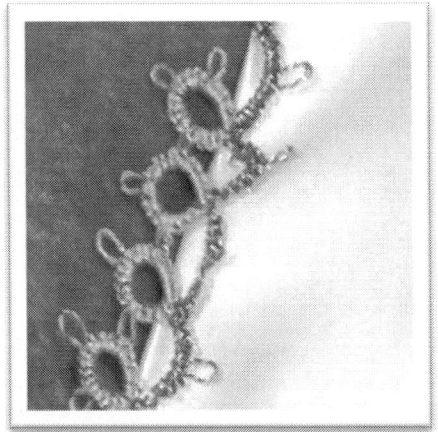

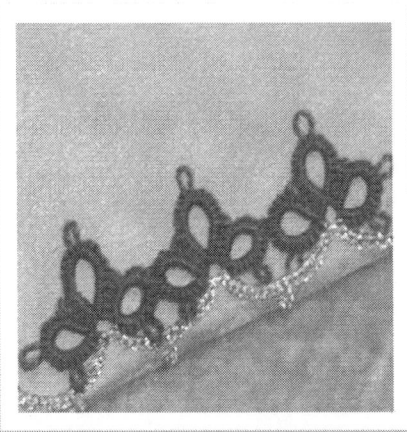

Project #1 Single Rings and Chains **Project #2 Trefoils and Chains**

Purpose: Learn to use a chain to join motifs
Learn about Reverse Work (RW)
Learn about adding threads
Learn how to vary a pattern
Practice joining rings
Practice reading a pattern

Materials: Crochet cotton or other thread in desired color or colors[31]
Tatting shuttle
Tape measure

Length: As long as needed to edge your project

Discussion:

As can be seen in the last lessons, the string space between rings or motifs is somewhat of a problem. Unless it can be used to accent some aspect of the project, it must be hidden in some way and its use is simply to

---

[31] Here the ball and shuttle threads need not be the same color, and some designs will work even more beautifully if they are not.

attach the lace to a project. As one gets more practiced with the art of doing correct double stitches on rings and chains, and with connecting rings on chains and between motifs with a picot-join, what seems a liability—the physical fact of spacing between motifs—can become an aspect of design. This can be done simply by combining chains and ring motifs.

By tying a ball and shuttle thread together, the tatter can create both a chain and a ring motif. The project can start with either the ring or the chain depending upon the pattern. Below a chain is started first. By setting aside the extra thread required to make the chain, the tatter then creates a ring as close to the end of the chain of double stitches as possible and proceeds according to the pattern instructions for the ring motif. The change from chain to ring usually requires the tatter to turn the chain over before starting the ring. In most patterns the instruction is "*reverse work*[32]" or simply RW.[33] There is no actual difference in how the stitches themselves are made and no other device keeps the stitches following the reverse in the new direction. The thread tends to "remember" the positions of the various stitches—probably as a result of areas of stretch and the absence of it—and an interruption of the work occurs which becomes part of the design. As can be seen in the photo below, reverse work causes the stitches and picots of the chain to point in the opposite direction of those in the ring.

Illustration of Reverse Work in Chains and Rings with Picots

Although there is no physical barrier to prevent the two from going the same

---

[32] See also Lesson 5.
[33] Reverse work as described here is a verb of command, not a noun. Reverse work as a descriptive noun is a technique that produces double stitches along the opposite thread on a ring in process; it creates the visual effect of two halves rather than a continuous ring.

direction, generally speaking the threads of the two "remember" the direction in which they were worked.

As usual, the rings are made entirely on the shuttle thread. Once the entire motif, as for instance the three petal motif in the previous lesson, is completed, the chain thread is taken up again. Here, too, the first double stitch of the chain is made as close to the base of the ring motif as possible, and the chain completed as per the pattern instructions. Imagine if you will that the linking threads of the motifs below were short chains of double stitches instead of unworked thread, and you will have the concept.

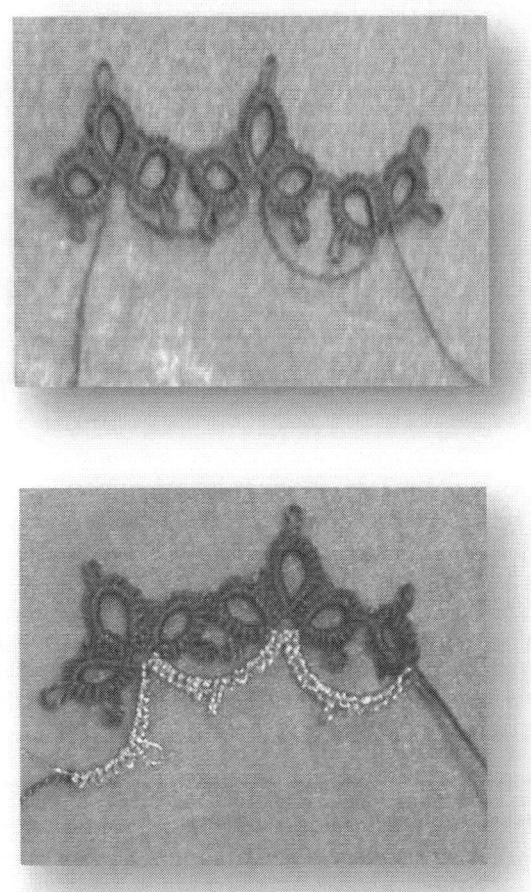

Three Petal Motif from Lesson 7 (top) and Variation with Chain (bottom)

Pattern 1:

Tie a ball and shuttle thread together.

Begin with a chain of 5 ds, p, 5 ds. Leaving the ball thread aside, reverse work.

Take the shuttle thread and arrange it around the hand in the position for making rings. Starting as close as possible to the last double stitch of the chain, begin the first ring.[34]

First Ring: 5 ds, 3 p sep by 5 ds, 5 ds, cl. RW.

*Chain: 5 ds, p, 5 ds. RW

Second Ring: 5 ds, j to last p of previous R, 5 ds, 2 p sep by 5 ds, 3 ds, cl. RW.*

Repeat between the stars until desired length.

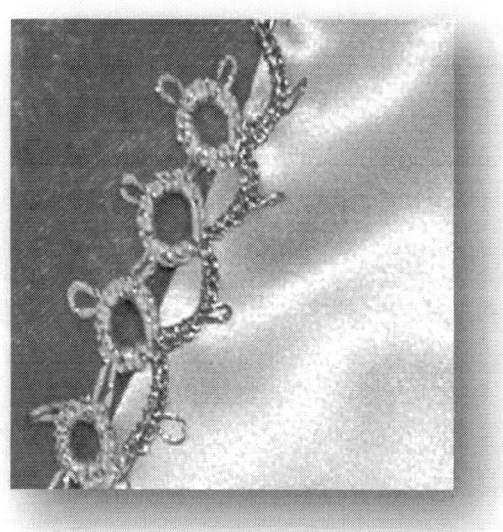

Satin with Gold Tatted Edging for Bride and Bride's Maids' Gowns

---

[34] In changing from the chain to the ring procedure, you will almost certainly require more thread from the shuttle. You can unwind what you need. In changing from the ring to the chain, however, you will need to rewind the shuttle thread to gain more control over it and to avoid mistaking the slack for the working thread, as using it this way will put knots in your work. With time and practice your fingers will come to "know" what is "too long" or "too short" by virtue of the tension required to complete the double stitch with the least effort. It is always wise to "listen" to what your fingers are telling you.

Even the simplest and least expensive satin fabric can be given a more elegant appearance by the addition of a tatted edging of rings and chains[35] or more complicated inserts in gold or silver threads.

Having learned the process of adding chains to rings with this simple edging, try the following more complex edging based on that from Lesson 7.

Pattern 2: Trefoil
Tie a ball and shuttle thread together.

> First Motif: Begin with a chain of 8 ds, p, 8 ds.[36] Leaving the ball thread aside, reverse work (RW), take the shuttle thread and arrange it around the hand in the position for making rings. Starting as close as possible to the last double stitch of the chain, begin the first ring of the first motif as follows:
> First Ring. 5 ds, 3 p sep. by 5 ds, 5 ds, cl.
> Second Ring. Starting at the base of the last ring, 5 ds, j to last
> p of last R, 6 ds, 2 p separated by 6 ds, 5 ds, cl.
> Third Ring. Starting at the base of the last ring, 5 ds, j to last p
> of last R, 5 ds, 2 p separated by 5 ds, 5ds, cl. RW. Starting as close as possible to the last double stitch of the previous chain, ch of 8 ds, p, 8 ds. RW. Starting as close as possible to the last double stitch of the chain, begin the second motif.
> Second Motif:
> > *First Ring. 5 ds, p, 5ds, j to the 2nd (middle) picot of the

---

[35] Note that this type of edging might also be used for button holes, with covered satin buttons passed either through the rings or through the loops made by the chains. This would be very effective as faux openings on sleeves or as an actual fastening on the back of a gown.

[36] If in the progress of your tatting you discover than the chain is too short to make your edging lie flat, you may add an extra double stitch to either side of the picot to extend the chain. This may happen if your ball and shuttle threads are different, in which even a slight difference in diameter may make the chain smaller—or larger—than the rings.

last ring of the last motif,[37] 5 ds, p, 5 ds, cl.

<u>Second Ring</u>. Starting at the base of the last ring, 5 ds, j to last p of last R, 6 ds, 2 p separated by 6 ds, 5ds, cl.

<u>Third Ring</u>. Starting at the base of the last ring, 5 ds, j to last p of last R, 5 ds, 2 p separated by 5 ds, 5ds, cl. RW. Starting as close as possible to the last double stitch of the previous chain,[38] ch of 8 ds, p, 8 ds. RW. Starting as close as possible to the last double stitch of the chain, begin the next motif.*

Continue the pattern between the stars (**) until the edging is the desired length.[39]

A casual examination of the completed edging in this pattern in the photo below reveals that there are actually a number of ways that even a relatively inexperienced tatter might change it into a new design. If you are looking for tatting uniquely and specifically you, never let the pattern stand in your way! Small changes and any corrections needed to make it work are well worth it.

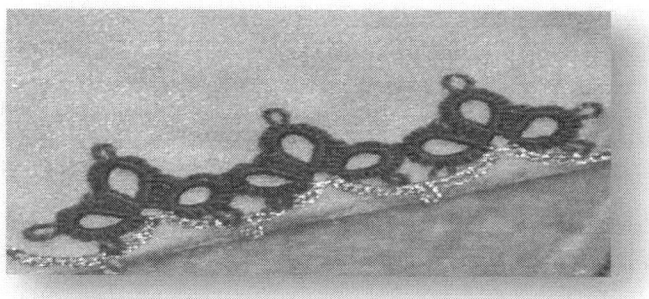

Appliqué Tatted Edging, Pattern 2, on Faux Suede

---

[37] Take care when joining the first ring of the second motif to the previous motif that you haven't rotated the previous motif, as this will create a twist in the position of the chains. The entire edging should be linear and flat throughout.

[38] Starting as close as possible to the chain that started the motif will make the chain appear more uniform and unbroken.

[39] With experience you will notice that the second, or continuing, motif and its associated chain actually encapsulate the pattern for this edging. Once you are comfortable with "reading" your work for the number of double stitches, picots and joins, you can leave your paper pattern behind if you carry your tatting with you to work or elsewhere. Without a cumbersome book of tatting patterns, the shuttle, ball and work-in-progress can easily fit into a handbag, sometimes even into a pocket.

Note, especially at this point, that in working ever more elaborate patterns your shuttle thread is going to be rapidly consumed in the process. You will find it expedient to have two balls of thread for many projects: one for the working ball thread and the other for replenishing your shuttle. If you know you are going to be making a lengthy edging—for instance for the opening of a pillow case, which can use up to 40 inches or more of lace of anywhere from one quarter to two inches in width—you may find it helpful to use the Tatsy Shuttle, which holds a larger amount of the standard sized threads. It will save you the task of splicing your new and old threads in the context of the project. This shuttle is somewhat more awkward to use for a beginner but may be worth getting used to for more ambitious projects.

There are several methods of splicing threads recommended in various tatting books, but I almost always end up using the simple method of avoiding them if I can by using a Tatsy Shuttle. If unavoidable, I tie the new thread to the old as close to the beginning of a chain or the end of a ring as I can. Adding them in the midst of a ring is virtually impossible since the ring will not close over the knot. If I expect to run out of thread in the middle of a ring, I add it at the base of the last chain or ring made. It is functionally hidden in the context of the pattern by this means, making it less noticeable. If the knot takes up a fair amount of space in the pattern, as it might with larger gauge threads, I may count it as one of my double stitches. Doing so prevents lopsidedness in the motif.

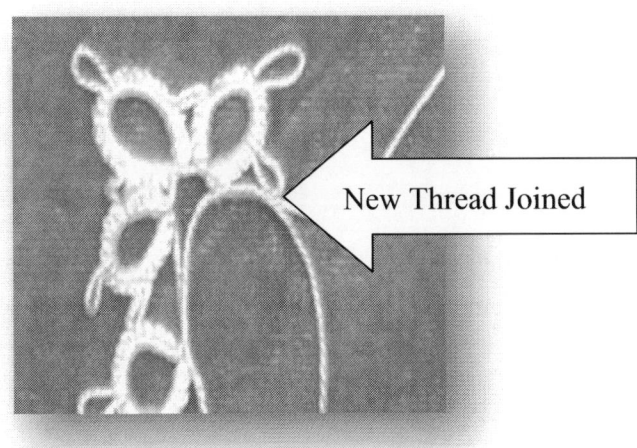

New Thread Tied on at the Base of a Ring

Using the basic square knot is the best method of tying, although an overhand knot may also work. To ensure that the knot does not become unfastened during the tatting process or from wear during use, I add a small amount of fast drying permanent glue to it before cutting the end threads as close as possible. As I said, however, other methods exist[40], including twisting old and new threads together and weaving the tail of the old thread back through the preceding double stitches to anchor it. Other sources suggest using sewing thread to smoothly bind the two against one another so that the new thread is functionally a continuation of the old one. Neither of these methods has worked well for me.

You may note that during the process of tatting, the shuttle thread becomes somewhat difficult to control, curling or not lying in useful loops over the hand thread. This may be because the thread has become overly twisted during use. To untwist the thread, simply let your shuttle dangle from the end of the thread; you will find that the shuttle rotates in one direction until the twist in the thread has been removed. It may then start turning in the opposite direction. At this point you can return to tatting again with increased control.

---

[40] Janette Baker presents some interesting and useful ideas in her book, *Learning to Tat*, which I will myself try.

Lesson 10: Alternate treatment of thread spaces—interweaving threads

Project: Bookmark

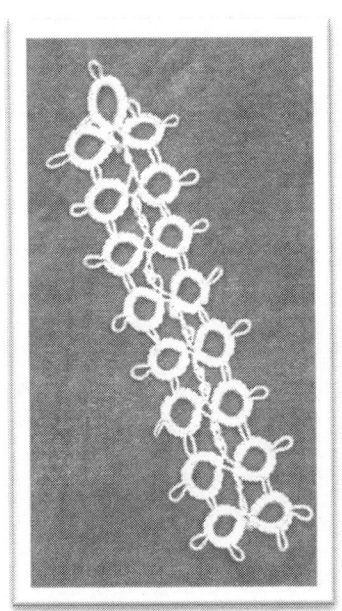

Bookmark, Insert, or Pendulum

Purpose: Learn to use shuttle "weaving" to join motifs
Practice reading a pattern
Materials: Crochet cotton or other thread in desired color
Tatting shuttle
Tape measure
Length: As long as needed to make the bookmark

Discussion:

One of my favorite patterns, a tatted bell, came with a kit accompanying my first Tatsy Shuttle. It was my first introduction to a method of combining motifs with the thread spaces between them by a form of weaving using the shuttle thread. Though in general I continue to prefer chains for the purpose, I still appreciate the cleverness of the technique and acknowledge the usefulness of the device. In fact, I still make most of my bells with this pattern and using this technique.

The technique here is a form of join, although instead of capturing a loop of thread through a picot, it is caught through the spacer thread between completed rings, and the same direction of pass is done at least twice. If the spacer thread is particularly long, as it may to space larger rings, several passes may be needed to evenly cover the spacer. Examine the following sequence of photos of a corner motif in nylon cord to understand how the process works.

First Parts of the Motif Completed

Loop of Shuttle Thread over Spacing Loop

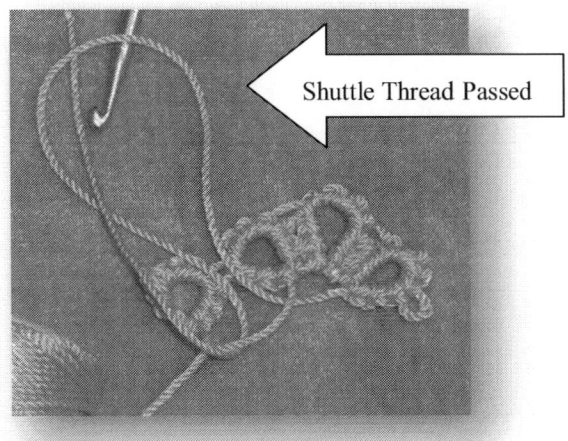

Shuttle Thread Passes Through the Loop

Completed Knot

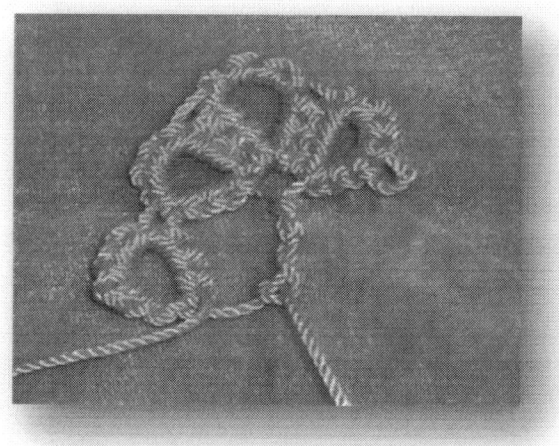

Three Completed Knots
(All passes are the same direction)

Finished Corner

Here the interweaving of the two spacer threads produces a stem for a triad of rings or "petals" while making the individual flanking rings into "leaves." The two free picots and the lower edge of the spacer threads can be used as a "sewing edge" to attach the corner motif to a project.

Practice Pattern (Flower and Leaf Motif above):

With shuttle, begin:

5 ds, p, 5ds, p, 5ds, close. Leave 1-1.5 inch length thread, then 5ds, j to last p of last ring, 5ds, p, 5ds, cl. Starting at the base of the last ring, 5ds, j to last p of last ring, 10ds, p, 5 ds, close. Starting at the base of the last ring, 5ds, j to p of last ring, 5ds, p, 5ds, close. Weave with 4 half stitches into the 1.5 inch open thread between the first "leaf" ring and the first "flower" ring. Leaving a half inch of thread after the woven area, begin 5ds, j to the last p of the last ring, 5ds, p, 5ds, close.

This can be used as a motif itself or it can be repeated as many times as necessary to make an edging.

Variation of the "Flower and Leaf" Motif on a Collar

Lesson Pattern: Bookmark[41]

Ring #1: R of 5 ds, 3 p sep by 5 ds, 5ds, cl.
Ring #2-8:[42] Leaving a thread space about a quarter to a half

---

[41] For practice, see if you can pick out the pattern for the corner motif in the picture above.

inch long, R of 5 ds, j to last p of prev R, 5 ds, 2 p sep by 5 ds, 5 ds, cl.

<u>Ring #9</u>: Starting at the base of the last ring, R of 5 ds, j to last p of prev R, 10ds, 2 p sep by 10ds, 5ds, cl.

<u>Ring #10</u>: Starting at the base of the last ring, R of 5ds, j to last p of prev R, 5 ds, 2 p sep by 5 ds, 5ds, cl.

<u>Ring #11-17</u>:[43] Weaving the shuttle thread around the thread space opposite and beginning the ring along the shuttle thread at the level of the ring opposite, R of 5 ds, j to last p of prev R, 5 ds, 2 p sep by 5 ds, 5 ds, cl.[44]

You may like to weave a narrow ribbon through the openings or glue a wider ribbon to the back to add color. You might add a row of fringe to the flat end or a single fringe, bell, bead or other item to the pointed end for emphasis.

---

[42] At this point, you may add as many of this type of ring as needed to achieve the length you desire.

[43] If you have added rings after #8, you will have to add rings after #17 in the pattern to balance this side of the bookmark.

[44] This bookmark has two different ends, but one with identical ends can be made with an additional technique appearing in the next lesson.

Lesson 11: Joining rings into a circle—the double twist.

Project: Daisy earrings, pin, (boutonniere or bouquet)

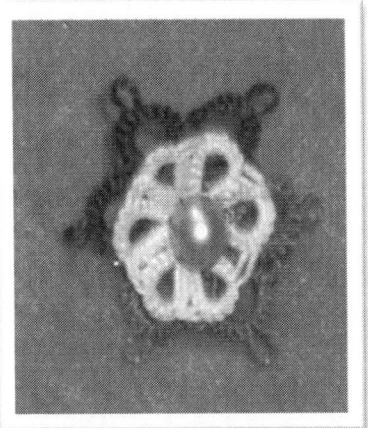

Purpose: Learn to join an end ring with a first ring to complete a round motif

Materials: Crochet cotton or other thread in desired color
Tatting shuttle
Appropriate jewelry findings

Discussion:

Completing a motif by joining a final ring with a beginning ring, as for daisies, is a little tricky. Treating it as a simple picot/join as it has already been learned will work, though it will generally create a noticeable twist in the joining picot. To avoid this, one does a double twist procedure that puts the picot in the proper orientation for the join such that it "untwists" itself open when it is complete.

To do the double twist, the first "petals" of the daisy are completed; then the final ring is finished to the point of the final join (see the next photo). The working ring is then held in position as usual, but the bulk of the finished motif is twisted to the left and over the left index finger, (see the photos following); this brings the picot to be joined into the range of the working ring.

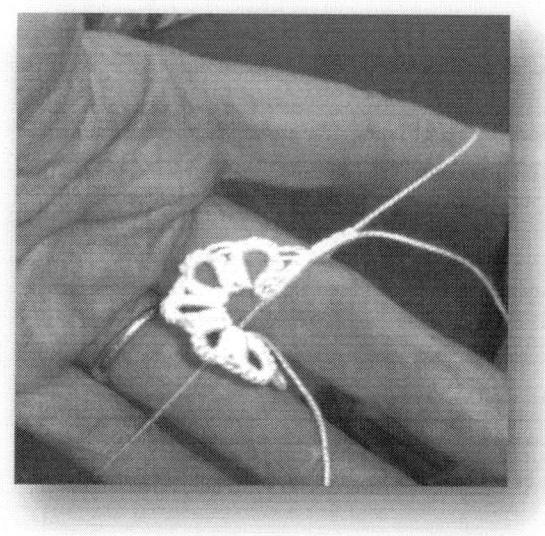

Five Rings Completed with Started Final Ring

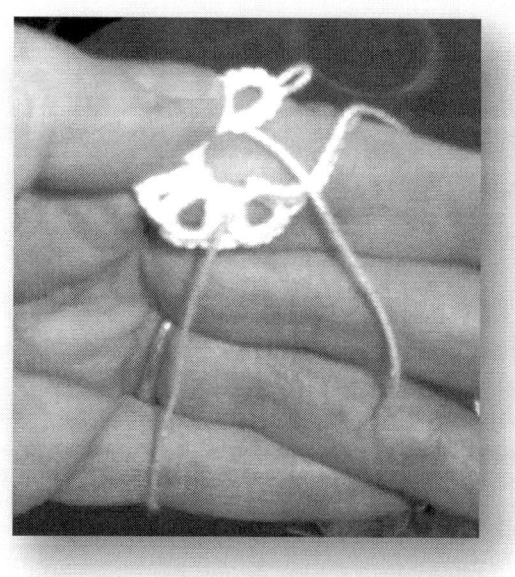

First Twist of Motif to the Left

To avoid the undesired twist of the joined picot in the finished motif, however, the end ring must be twisted to the left once again, bringing the joining picot to within range of the working thread.

If you examine the photo below, you will see that the closed end of the first ring is now facing away from the working thread; additionally the tail that began the motif is pointing up and to the left, while the picot to be joined is now upside down but still within range of the working thread of the finishing ring. The join is then completed as usual, with a loop of the working thread drawn up from below, and the shuttle passed up through it as usual. The second half of the picot/join is then completed, and the pattern finished as directed. By joining and cutting the tail and shuttle threads the motif is ready for use in your project.

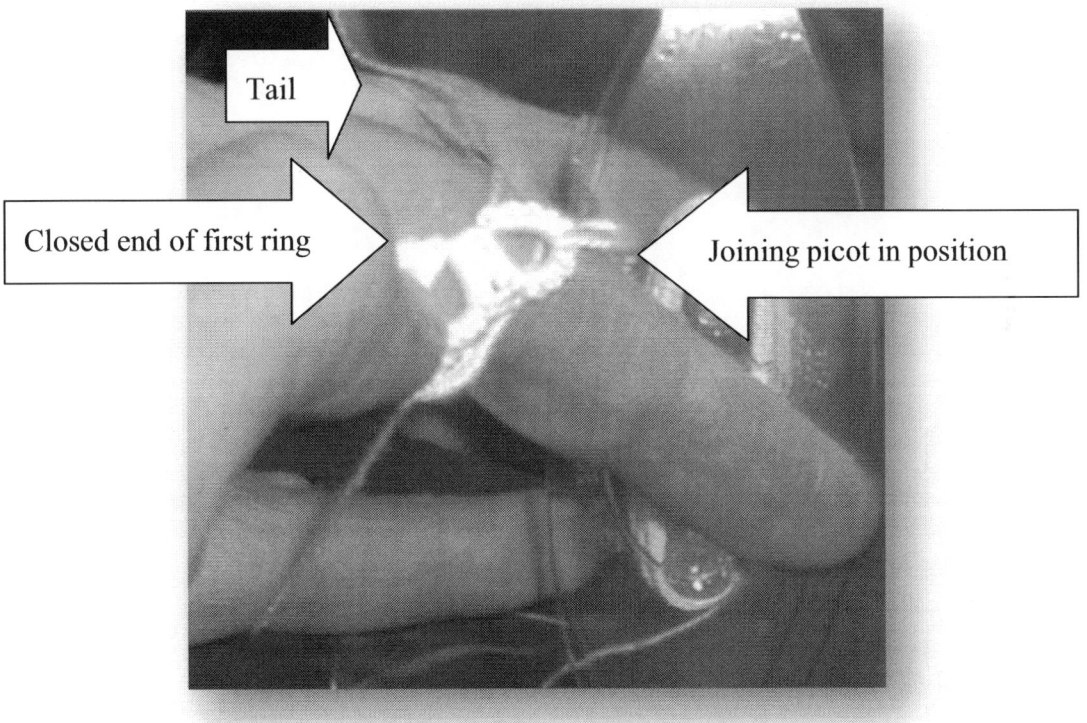

**Second Twist of End Ring to the Left,
Aligning Joining Picot**

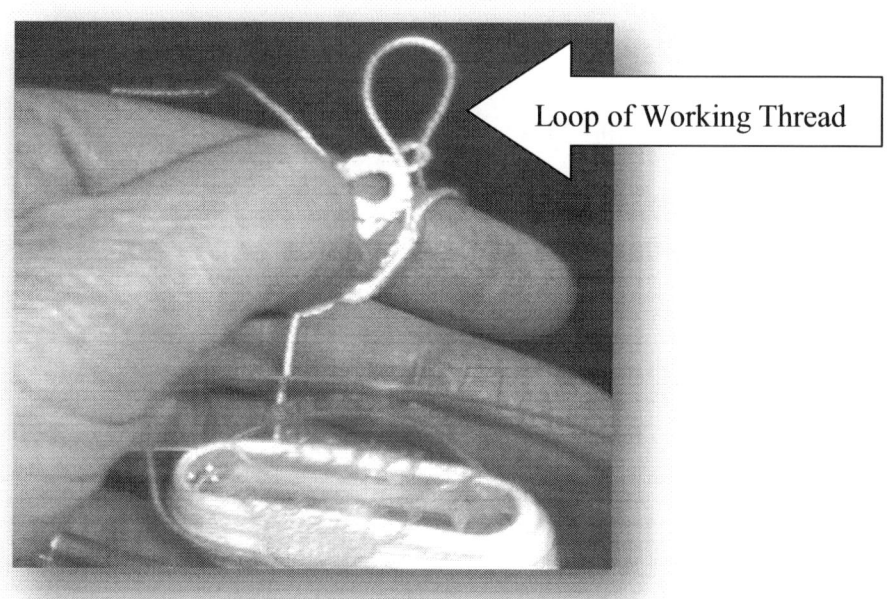

Working Thread Loop for the Join

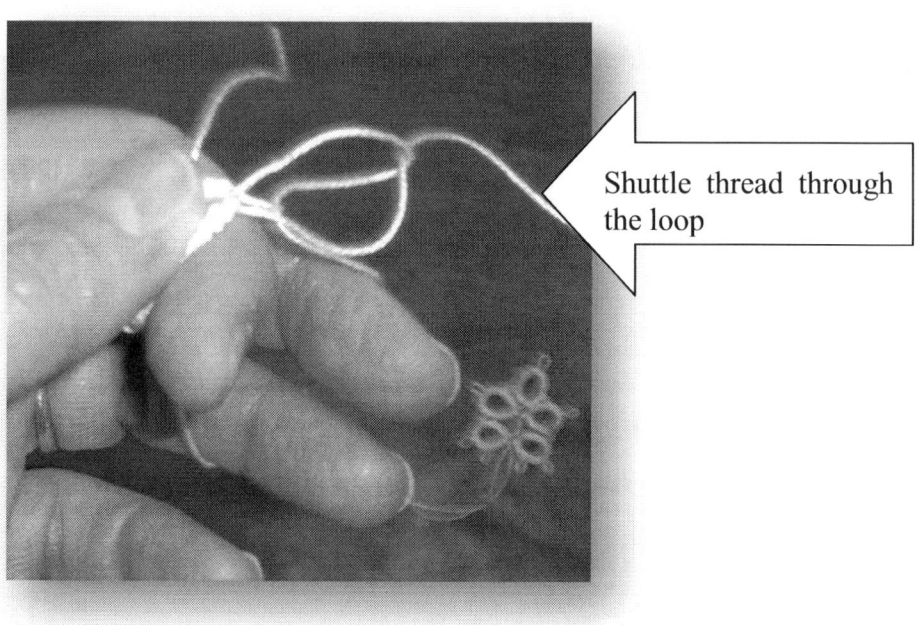

Shuttle Pass through Joining Loop

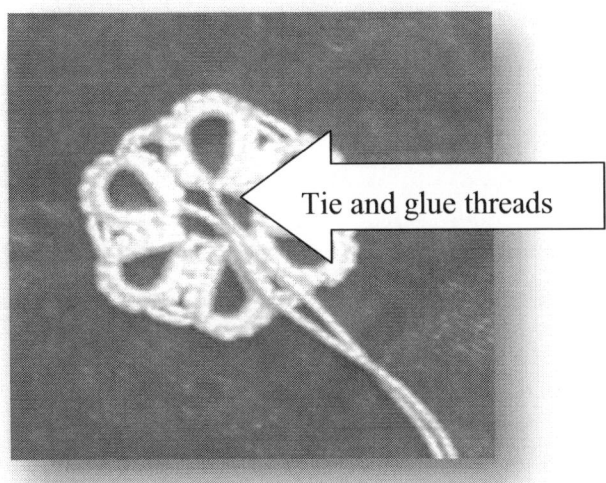

Finished Join and Motif

Pattern 1: Daisy earrings or pin

Daisy with Pearl Bead Center and Earring Wire

With shuttle thread, R 5ds, 2 p sep by 5 ds, 5ds, cl.[45] *R

---

[45] It will help if you pull your rings as tightly closed as possible before starting the next ring. There is almost always a small space that arises between succeeding rings during the tatting process. By closing tightly then relaxing each ring after succeeding rings are started, this space can be eliminated.

5 ds, j to last p of prev R, 5 ds, p, 5 ds, cl.* Repeat ** 4 times. R 5 ds, j to last p of prev R, 5 ds, j to first picot of first R (using the double twist as above), 5 ds, cl. Tie threads and cut. Add pin back or earring wires as indicated.

Be aware that few patterns will actually ask for a "double twist technique" or give you instructions that direct you in the process. You will almost certainly have to remember for yourself that when you join the final ring of a circular motif to the beginning ring, you must twist the motif to the left twice to achieve a perfect join.[46]

Pattern 2: Daisy earrings or pin

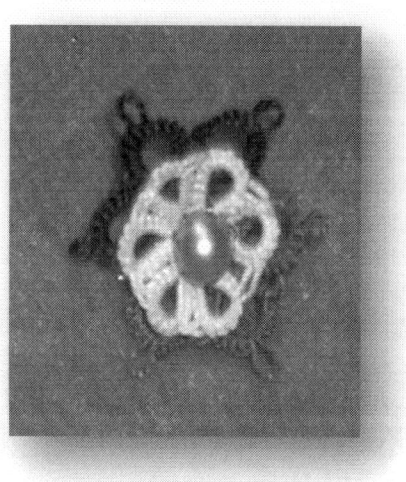

Outer Daisy:

With shuttle thread in first color: R 5ds, 3 p sep by 5 ds, 5ds, cl. *R[47] 5 ds, j to last p of prev R, 5 ds, 2 p sep by 5 ds, 5 ds, cl.* Repeat ** a total of 4 times. R 5 ds, j to last p of prev R, 5 ds, p, 5 ds, j to first picot of first R (using the double twist as

---

[46] For years I struggled with twisted picots at the ends of motifs, until I ran across a pattern that actually told me how to avoid them. As I recall, one of the Tatsy kit patterns gave the instructions but did not name the technique. I labeled it a "double twist" to mark it as a unique join technique.

[47] Notice that there is no longer an instruction to start at the base of the previous ring. This is usually a given in most patterns. When and if a space is required, that fact and the size will be expressly indicated in the pattern.

above), 5 ds, cl. Tie threads, cut, and glue.

Center Daisy:
With shuttle thread in second color: R 5ds, 2 p sep by 5 ds, 5ds, cl.[48] *R 5 ds, j to last p of prev R, 5 ds, p, 5 ds, cl.* Repeat ** 4 times. R 5 ds, j to last p of prev R, 5 ds, j to first picot of first R (using the double twist as above), 5 ds, cl. Tie threads, cut and glue.

Finishing:
Center the daisies over one another, sewing or wiring a bead at the center. Add pin back or earring wires as indicated.

As you can easily see, this pattern is simply a variant of the previous one, adding a single decorative picot flanked by 5 double stitches to centers of the rings of the outer motif. Try varying the number of double stitches, picots, and/or rings for other daisy arrangements.

Pattern 3: Daisy boutonniere or bouquet

Make one each or more of daisy patterns one and two in three to seven rings and in one or several colors. Stack the daisies together. Measure and cut a florists' wire to the necessary length. After attaching a bead to one end of the wire, thread it through the center openings in the daisies from front to back. For a boutonniere add a gathered net or other fabric to the back of these. Wrap the wire with florists' tape, binding in fabric leaves along the stem if desired. For a bouquet, make several flowers with leaves and stems and form an arrangement for a small vase or for the decoration of a gift package.

---

[48] Notice that not all patterns will remind you to start the succeeding rings close to the base of the first in a situation where it should be apparent by virtue of the design.

Lesson 12: Adding beads to rings

Project: Daisy with beads

Daisy with Beads

Purpose: Learn to add beads to rings
Materials: Crochet cotton or other thread in desired color
Tatting shuttle
Appropriate jewelry findings

Discussion:

Adding beads to rings is nearly identical to adding them to chains. In both cases, the bead or other embellishment occupies the thread space of a picot in the motif in progress and is kept in place by the double stitches that precede and follow it. Also in both cases, the beads to be added to the project are first strung onto the thread before beginning the project. Because the ring involves only the shuttle thread, however, all of the beads required for the project need to be wound onto it until needed for placement. This means that, whereas the beads of a chain can be numerous and of any size—because they are out of the way on the ball thread—those on a shuttle thread must be rather small or the shuttle rather large. This imposes a limit on the sizes and types of beads that can be added. Given that most rings are small themselves, however, this need not be an obstacle to employing the technique.

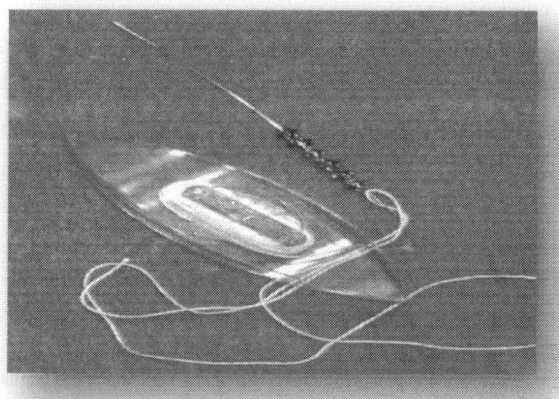

Adding Beads to the Shuttle Thread with a Beading Needle

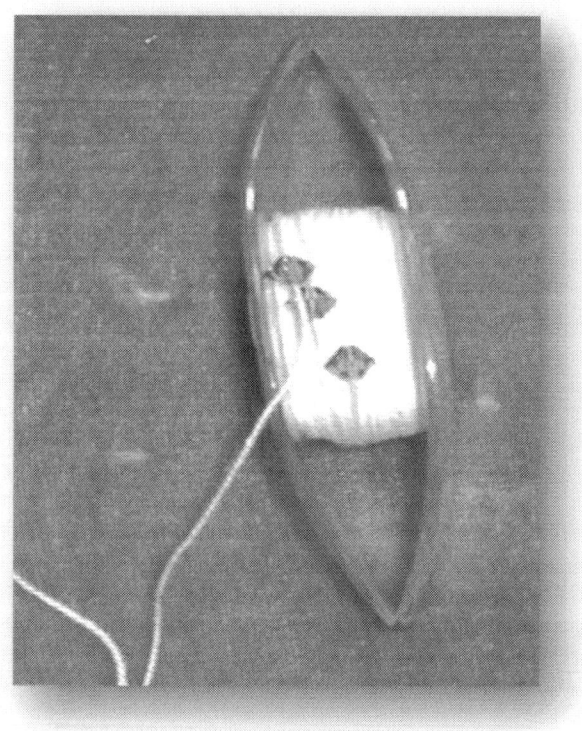

Threaded Beads Wound onto the Shuttle

One further caveat in the beading process in the case of rings is important. The bead or beads required for a given ring can be moved either from the hand thread or from the shuttle thread, depending upon the effect desired. If they are moved onto the thread around the hand until placed, the bead is on the working thread rather than on the base thread and ensures that the ornament remains above the completed ring rather than inside of it.

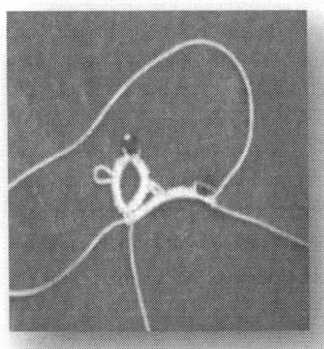

Placement from the Hand puts the Bead on the Picot above the Base Thread

Leaving the beads on the shuttle and moving them into place as needed from this direction will produced the opposite effect; the bead will be below the working thread and inside the ring.

Placement from the Shuttle puts the Bead on the Base Thread and inside the Picot

This is a design decision pure and simple. Some rings may actually look better with the bead pointing to the center of the ring. A dependant pearl might look better this way, for instance. Alternating the techniques, with one bead outside of a ring and one inside the next might also prove profitable.

The photographs below demonstrate the process of placing a bead on the working thread from the hand.

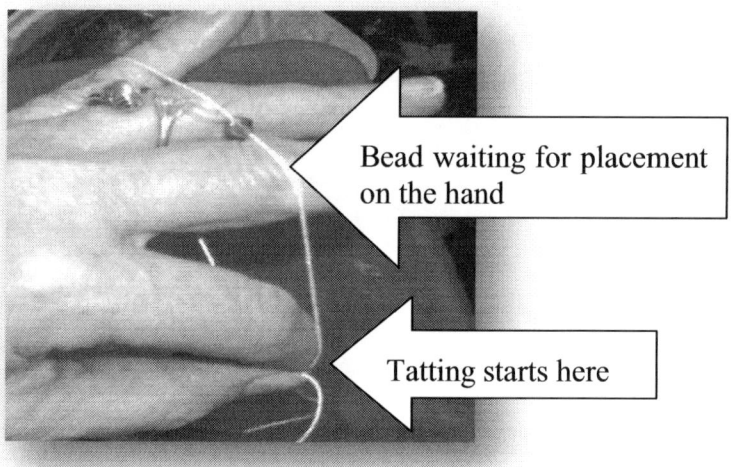

Bead Moved into Position for Placement

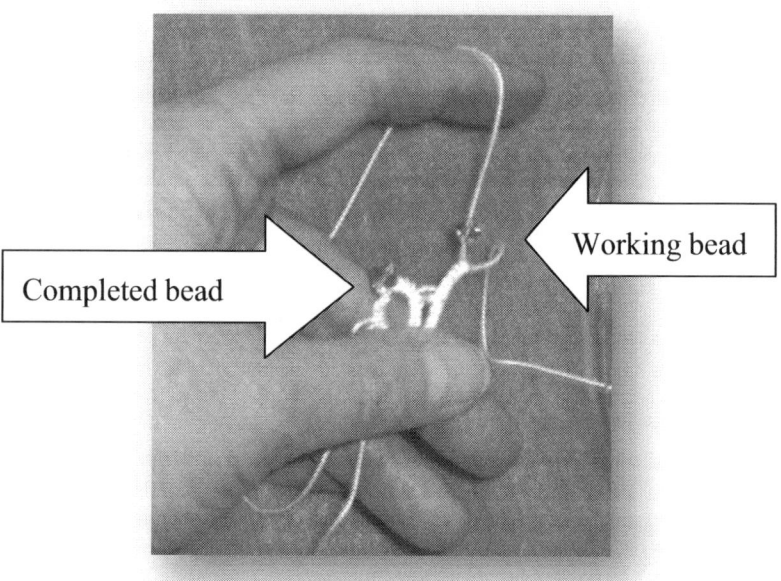

Bead Being Positioned between Double Stitches

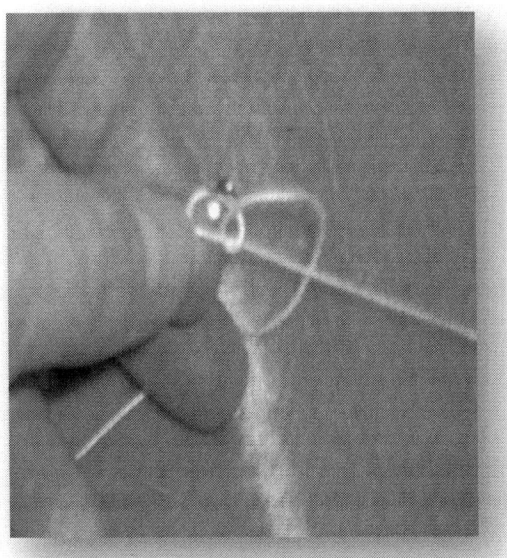

Beginning of Closing Double Stitch after Bead Placement

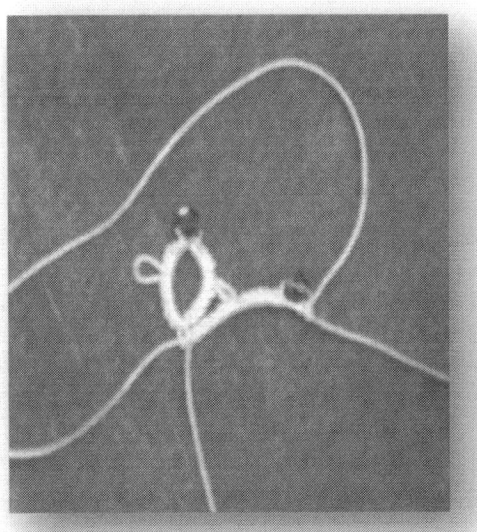

Completed Ring and Partial Ring with Beads in Place.

Notice, here, that the bead is part of the picot on the working thread and not on the base thread at all. The base thread helps support the bead above the ring of double stitches. Had you wanted the bead to be inside the ring, the bead would have been slid into position from the shuttle rather than the hand, and the double stitch completed as usual. This would have placed the bead on the base thread with the working thread above it, causing the bead to point down to the center of the completed ring (see above and also examples below).

Pattern: Daisy with beads

Prepare the shuttle with the required number of beads (here 6)[49] on the tail end of the thread and rewind beads and thread onto the shuttle.

With shuttle thread, move one bead to the working thread on the hand , then: R 6ds, p, 6 ds, bead, 6ds, p, 6 ds cl. *Moving another bead to the left hand, R 6 ds, j to last p of prev R, 6 ds, bead, 6 ds, p, 6 ds, cl.* Repeat ** 3 times. Bead to the left hand, R 6 ds, j to last p of prev R, 6 ds, bead, 6 ds, j to first picot of first R (using the double twist technique), 6 ds, cl. Sliding the last bead to the center on the shuttle thread, tie it in place with the tail thread, glue and cut. Add pin back or earring wires as desired.

Try the same pattern moving the individual beads from the shuttle rather than placing them on the hand for each ring. Compare the effects so that you can make design decisions in the future based upon what you know about both techniques.   Here are some examples of base thread bead placements. Notice that this type of placement has a "front" and "back" aspect which should be taken into consideration when making your design choices.

---

[49] Note that there is no reason that two or more beads could not be added to picot spaces of the motif to create different effects.

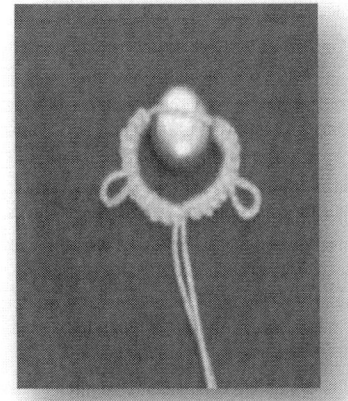 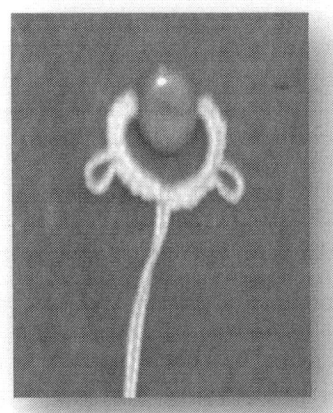

Flat Bead, (Front, right. Back, left)

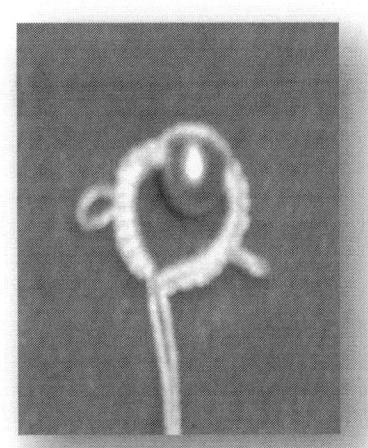 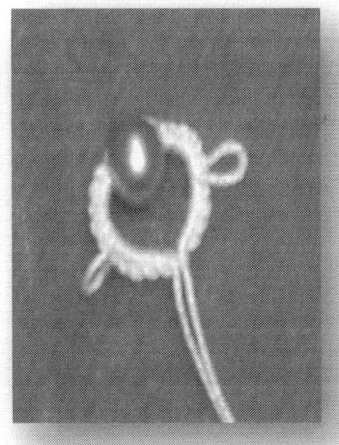

Round Bead, (Front, right. Back, left.)

Lesson 13: Joining individual motives—longer and larger projects

Project: Joined motifs

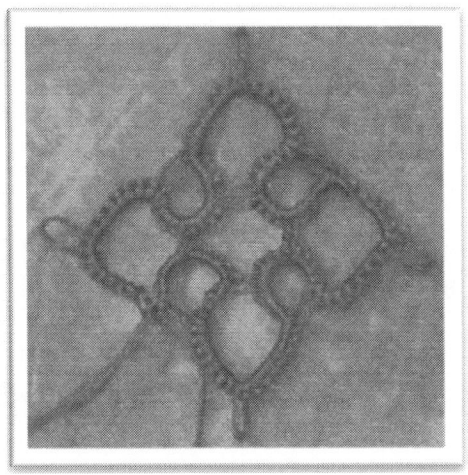

Purpose: Learn to join motifs into larger projects
Learn about personal working tension and how to make a uniform set of motifs
Materials: Crochet cotton or other thread in desired color
Tatting shuttle

Discussion:

Larger projects are usually a matter of joining a number of individual motifs. This is accomplished by joining one in progress into the appropriate available picots of a previously completed one (or ones). Any number may be combined in this way to achieve products of a variety of sizes and uses, from edgings and doilies to table cloths and bedspreads. Notice that this is the *tatter's* way of creating a larger project. Other ways they might be joined is by crocheted bands or with ribbons or other materials.

In making a larger project in this way, care must be exerted to keep each motif as uniformly like the others as possible. Just as with knitting, there is a degree of individuality to the tension that each person brings to tatting and also a characteristic degree that this tension changes during the working process. To make certain that your motifs fit together properly, it is important to know when you need to "loosen up" or "tighten up" your handwork to produce the desired effect.

Joined Square Motifs:

Tie the shuttle & ball threads together. Note that all picots should be generous. It will help to keep all double stitches on the corners (the 8ds) loose and those in the loops (the 5ds) tighter. Doing so will make the design clearer and the working process more apparent.[50]

Basic Motif:

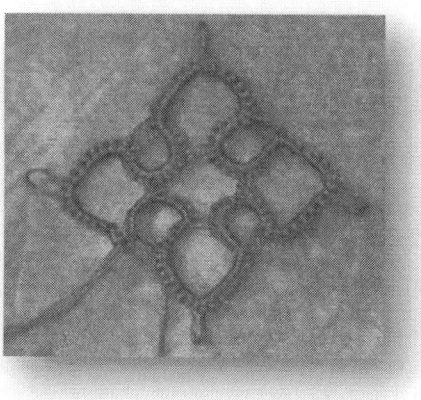

Start the chain beginning with a p, using the knot of the ball and shuttle threads as the first "ds" forming it, then 8ds [remembering that the second of the ds for the p counts as the

---

[50] This is the same motif as described in Lesson 5 starting on page 47. Refer to it for photographs making clearer the process of working it

1st of the 8], p, 8ds, p, [1st corner made].

Reverse work (RW). 5ds, p, 5ds, p, 5ds [1st interior loop made].

RW. j to the 3rd p[51] from the beginning [which joins 2nd corner to the 1st], 8ds, p, 8ds, p [2nd corner made].

RW. 5ds, j to 4th free p from beg [the second p on the 1st loop], 5ds, p, 5ds [2nd interior loop made].

RW. j to 5th free p [the last p made on the 2nd corner] from beg [joins 3rd corner to 2nd], 8ds, p, 8ds, p [3rd corner made].

RW. 5 ds, j to second p on the 2nd loop, 5ds, p, 5ds [3rd interior loop].

RW. j to last p made on the 3rd corner [joins the 4th corner to the 3rd], 8 ds, p, 8 ds [4th corner made], j to first picot of the first corner [closing the motif at the corners].

RW. 5 ds, j to last free p of previous (3rd) interior loop, 5ds, j to the remaining free picot of the 1st interior loop, 5 ds, cut and tie thread onto the starting threads of the chain [completing the 4th interior loop].

If your intention is to make a **diamond edging** of these patterns, the instructions for the second and succeeding motifs are as follows:

Having completed the first square motif, start the chain of the next motif by beginning with a p, using the knot of the ball and shuttle threads as the first "ds" forming it, then 8ds, j to any available picot on the edge of the previous motif [linking this and the new one together], 8 ds, p [1st corner made].

Reverse work (RW). 5ds, p, 5ds, p, 5ds [1st interior loop made].

RW. j to the 3rd p from the beginning [which joins 2nd

---

[51] If you have followed the suggestions at the beginning of the instructions, the joining picot should be readily apparent at each point a join is required.

corner to the 1st], 8ds, p, 8ds, p [2nd corner made].

RW. 5ds, j to 4th free p from beg [the second p on the 1st loop], 5ds, p, 5ds [2nd interior loop made].

RW. j to 5th free p [the last p made on the 2nd corner] from beg [joins 3rd corner to 2nd], 8ds, p, 8ds, p [3rd corner made].

RW. 5 ds, j to second p on the 2nd loop, 5ds, p, 5ds [3rd interior loop].

RW. j to last p made on the 3rd corner [joins the 4th corner to the 3rd], 8 ds, p, 8 ds [4th corner made], j to first picot of the first corner [closing the motif at the corners].

RW. 5 ds, j to last free p of previous (3rd) interior loop, 5ds, j to the remaining free picot of the 1st interior loop, 5 ds, cut and tie thread onto the starting threads of the chain [completing the 4th interior loop].

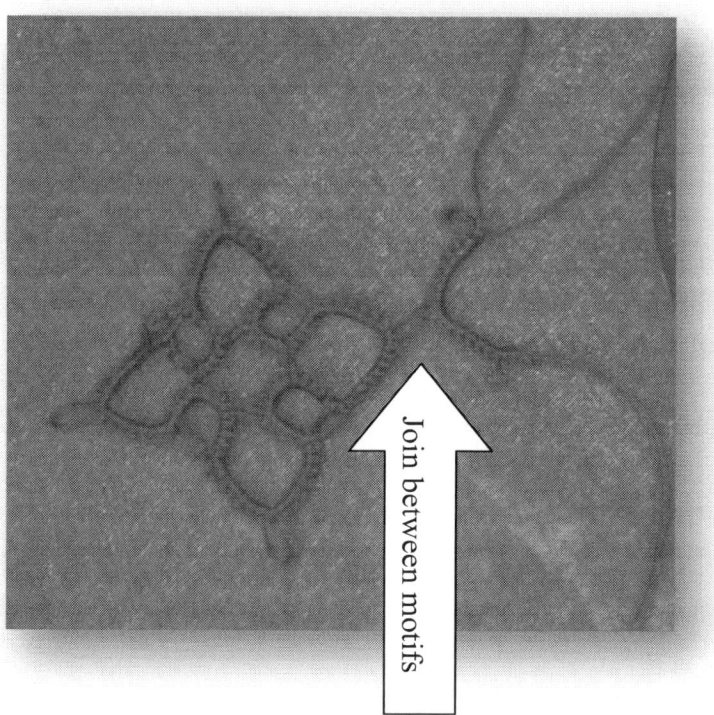

Beginning of Point to Point Join for Square Motif

If your intention is to make a **square edging** of these motifs the instructions for the second and succeeding motifs are as below:

Having completed the first square motif, start the chain of the next motif by beginning with a p, using the knot of the ball and shuttle threads as the first "ds" forming it, then 8ds, j to any available picot on the edge of the previous motif [linking this and the new one together], 8 ds, p [1st corner made].

Reverse work (RW), 5ds, p, 5ds, p, 5ds [1st interior loop made].

RW, j to the 3rd p from the beginning [which joins 2nd corner to the 1st], 8ds, j to the next adjacent p of the previous motif [linking the two motifs together at two sites, and producing a band of squares], 8ds, p [2nd corner made].

RW, 5ds, j to 4th free p from beg [the second p on the 1st loop], 5ds, p, 5ds [2nd interior loop made].

RW, j to 5th free p [the last p made on the 2nd corner] from beg [joins 3rd corner to 2nd], 8ds, p, 8ds, p [3rd corner made].

RW, 5 ds, j to second p on the 2nd loop, 5ds, p, 5ds [3rd interior loop].

RW, j to last p made on the 3rd corner [joins the 4th corner to the 3rd], 8 ds, p, 8 ds [4th corner made], j to first picot of the first corner [closing the motif at the corners].

RW, 5 ds, j to last free p of previous (3rd) interior loop, 5ds, j to the remaining free picot of the 1st interior loop, 5 ds, cut and tie thread onto the starting threads of the chain [completing the 4th interior loop].

As can be seen by comparison, the simple choice of a single or a double join between the motifs creates either a point-to-point diamond edging or a side-to-side band of squares.

If your intention is to make a **four-square or greater**:

The instructions for the third and fourth motifs are much the same as those above with additional joins connecting to picots as indicated in the process of joining the motifs for the larger work. Here too your design will involve the choice between a point-to-point or a side-to-side join for the project. The point-to-point technique using four "diamonds" can produce a larger, more open and airy design, since vacant diamond shaped areas can arise between the joined motifs. A side-to-side arrangement of "squares," on the other hand, will create a more massed effect and tend to produce a smaller project.

Even larger projects are possible, the size being more a matter of the patience of the tatter than of any limitations of technique, which remains the same. For those who like to carry their projects around with them, about half of the total number of the motifs required for the completed project can be worked separately, after which these may be joined by tatting them together with intervening motifs. An additional benefit of doing the project this way is that individual completed motifs may be compared with one another to ensure uniformity before joining them to one another.

The process is similar for combining round motifs—the patterns for which are actually more common.

Below are the instructions for the daisy motifs learned in Lesson 11.

Joined Daisy Motifs:

Basic Pattern:

With shuttle thread: R 5ds, 3 p sep by 5 ds, 5ds, cl. *R 5 ds, j to last p of prev R, 5 ds, 2 p sep by 5 ds, 5 ds, cl.* Repeat ** 4 times. R 5 ds, j to last p of prev R, 5 ds, p, 5 ds, j to first picot of first R (using the double twist as above), 5 ds, cl. Tie threads and cut.

Second and Succeeding Motifs for an Edging:

With shuttle thread: R 5ds, p, 5 ds, j to any free p of previous daisy motif, 5ds, p, 5ds, cl. *R 5 ds, j to last p of prev R [note that it is the last ring and not the previous motif], 5 ds, 2 p sep by 5 ds, 5 ds, cl.* Repeat ** 4 times. R 5 ds, j to last p of prev R, 5 ds, p, 5 ds, j to first picot of first R (using the double twist as above), 5 ds, cl. Tie threads and cut.

Daisies with Point to Point Joins

Daisies with Side to Side Joins

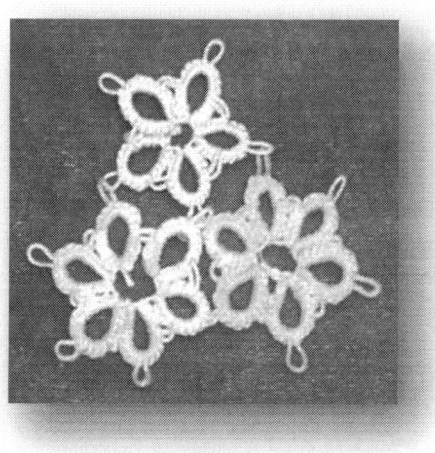

Daisy Motif with Two Sizes of Daisy
(With Possible Join Sites Indicated by Placement)

As can be seen, with round motifs, the choices are often a little more limited, depending upon the size and shape of the daisies or other motifs and upon whether all the rounds are the same size. The latter need not be the case, and some very elaborate patterns have been created using rounds of two or more sizes. Using several of the same size with two to four connections to one another will produce a more open work, while using two or more sizes will fill in open spaces creating a more massed effect. Often times table cloths, table runners, and placemats are made in the former style, while bed spreads are created in the latter. The choice, however, is yours.

PART THREE:
Details

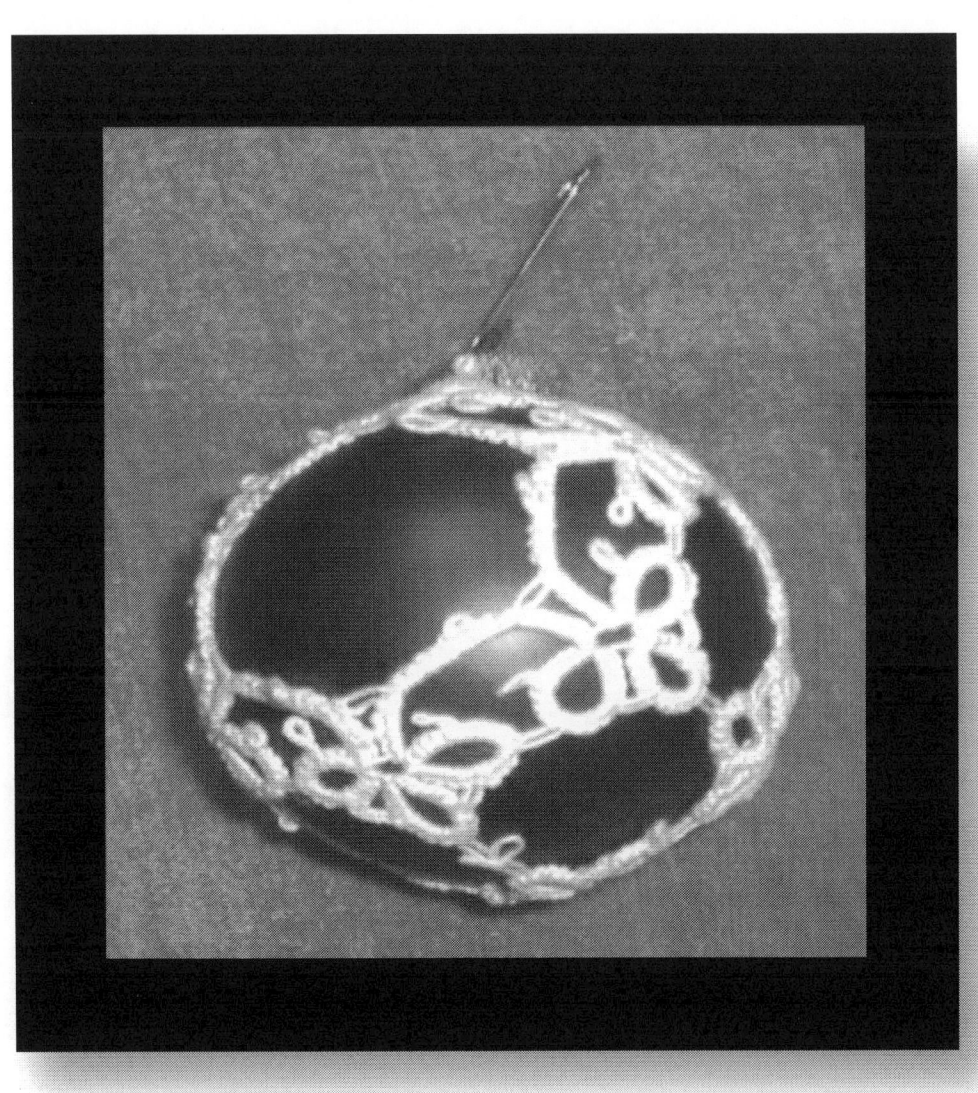

Lesson 14: Putting it all together

Purpose: Learn to create more elaborate patterns using picots, chains and ring motifs

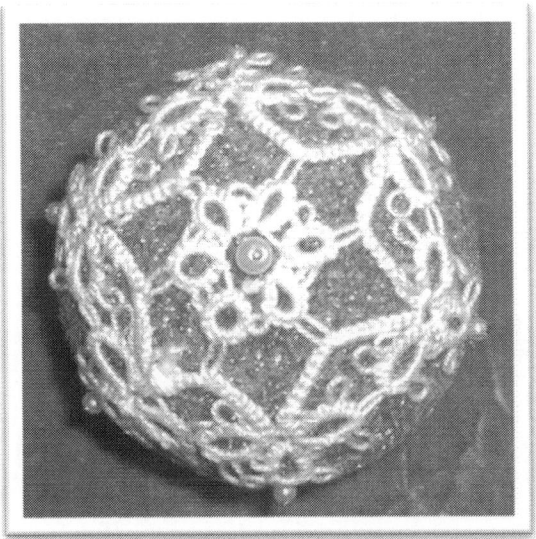

Materials: Crochet cotton or other thread in desired color
Tatting shuttle

Discussion:

Whether you realize it or not, by this lesson you have all the information and technique you require to create lovely designs of your own. Simply by varying the motifs above—trefoils, daisies, chains, squares, and so on—and combining them with one another, the student can produce a variety of different edgings and other projects.[52]

Included in this lesson are photographs illustrating some of the design possibilities which build on information in the above lessons. They are grouped in "families" of designs to show how they grow with changes. These are provided as teaching tools that suggest how a motif might go from one style to

---

[52] See also the Appendix, Decision List: The creative bit.

another. Understand, however, that your own ideas will add further to the possible changes in design.

Adding Petals and Picots:

Below are illustrations of some of the possible variations on the daisy motif. Notice that a change in the number of double stitches on the rings, the number of the rings themselves, or the number and density of picots on the rings produces markedly different results in each case.

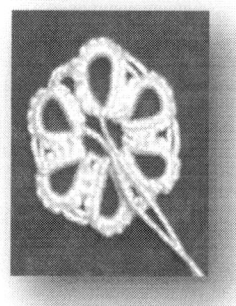  

Variations on the Daisy Pattern

Here are the patterns for all three. Study them to see the differences among them.

1. 6-Petal Daisy:
With shuttle thread, R 5ds, 2 p sep by 5 ds, 5ds, cl.[53] *R 5 ds, j to last p of prev R, 5 ds, p, 5 ds, cl.* Repeat ** 4 times. R 5 ds, j to last p of prev R, 5 ds, j to first picot of first R (using the double twist as above),[54] 5 ds, cl. Tie threads and cut.

2. 5-Petal Daisy with Picots:
With shuttle thread, R 5ds, 3 p sep by 5 ds, 5ds, cl. *R 5 ds, j to last p of prev R, 5 ds, 2p separated by 5 ds, 5 ds, cl.*

---

[53] It will help if you pull your rings as tightly closed as possible before starting the next ring. There is almost always a small space that arises between succeeding rings during the tatting process. By closing tightly then relaxing each ring after succeeding rings are started, this space can be eliminated.

[54] See chapter 11 if you've forgotten how to do this.

Repeat ** 2 more times. R 5 ds, j to last p of prev R, 5 ds, p, 5ds, j first picot of first R (using the double twist as above), 5 ds, cl. Tie threads and cut.

3. 5-Petal Daisy with 10 Picots:

With shuttle thread, R 5ds, 12 p sep by 1ds, 5ds, cl. *R 5 ds, j to last p of prev R, 1 ds, 11p separated by 1ds, 5 ds, cl.* Repeat ** 2 more times. R 5 ds, j to last p of prev R, 1 ds, 10p separated by 1ds, 1ds, j to first picot of first R (using the double twist as above), 5 ds, cl. Tie threads and cut.

As can be seen in these patterns there are only a few key points where variations occur, but these make all the difference to the overall effect of each design. Try making one of each and fasten them to a memo (see example on the next page) of some kind to keep them as type specimen for later reference. (See the Appendix for a form to copy).

Example of Notes on a Motif

Type Specimen: <u>5-petal, 10-picot daisy</u>   **Date:** <u>9/29/2009</u>

Notes regarding thread used.

White cotton crochet thread, size 20.

Pattern Notes (Sources, changes made, uses to which it was put, etc.)

Own pattern. 10 picots separated with 1 double stitch, and joins. Christmas ornaments, gift decorations and Christmas cards. Sugar starched to stiffen. Original number made: 37.

Adding Chains:

Somewhat more elaborate patterns can be created by combining motifs and/or by adding chains to them. Below is a basic pattern of joined trefoil motifs given on page 88 and as it was subsequently expanded on page 93.

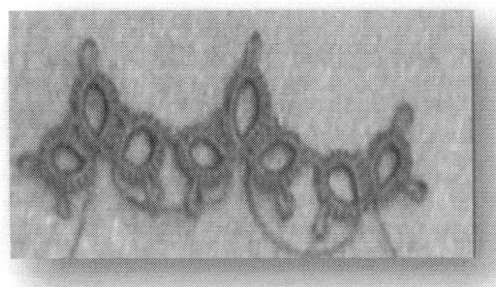

Basic Trefoil

Trefoil with Chain

The addition of the chains will allow the edging to stand away from whatever object or material to which it is applied, making it more prominent and adding width to the embellishment.

Adding Rows of Motives:

As the next illustration shows, this same trefoil with chains has now been expanded by adding a 6-petal daisy to pairs of trefoils by means of joins to picots in three places. This can add not only interest to a design but motif height as well. An edging that may start out only about one half to one inch might by this means expand to almost two or two and a half, making it more imposing and giving it a greater usefulness; from a pillowcase edging to a bridal gown edging, for instance.

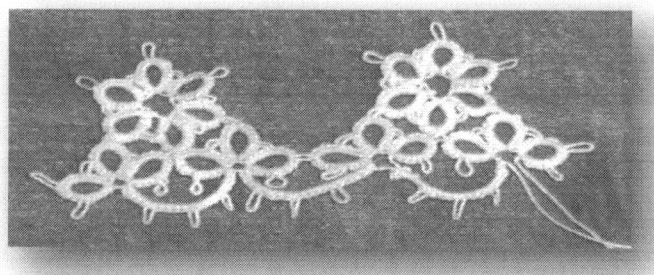

Trefoil and Chains with 6-petal Daisies.

Here is the same edging with an extra daisy bridging two of those in the previous row. As can be seen by this maneuver, the additional daisy not only adds itself to the motif but also creates a centered heart shape beneath it by virtue of the empty space whose shape it helps define.

Trefoil and Chains with 6-petal Daisies and Central Daisy Bridge and Heart Shape

This pattern might make a nice edging for a table cloth if expanded in length or serve as an insert motif into the corners of a table cloth or of placemats. Here again the overall width of the edging may reach up to three and half or four inches.

Though the above patterns may look very elaborate, there is nothing about them that even a practiced beginner couldn't manage providing they have the patience and the amount of time needed for the endeavor. Over the course of the book the student will already have done the same patterns; now they are merely conjoined.

Changing Directions with Joins

Here is a pattern that while it looks different really is not. If one were to lay it out straight without its numerous joins, it would actually reveal itself for what it is: a rather simple edging of quatrefoils and trefoils joined by chains. Here elaboration is created by joining several linear edging motifs to one another, introducing complexity and width without having to add separate medallions to the motif as was done in the previous cases.

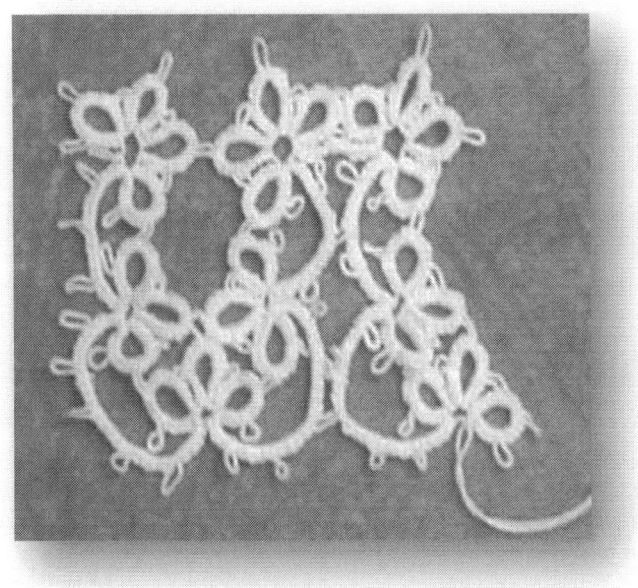

Trefoil and Quatrefoil Edging

Notice that this starts (in the upper left hand corner) with a quatrefoil followed by a trefoil bridged by a join and a chain and continues in a sinuous fashion up and down by the means of joins. All the tatter is doing is making a long chain of quatrefoils and trefoils with chains, as for a standard edging, but then he or she joins some of the motifs in from one to three places, causing the edging to turn corners. Study the above edging until you understand where the complexity arises.

As you can no doubt guess, this is an edging that will take considerable time to complete. By using much of the linear edging to create height instead of length, the overall length desired to finish a project will take longer. While one might have had up to eight inches of finished lace edging in the above sample had it had remained in its linear form, here it will probably be more like four or five, the extra inches having disappeared into the increase in height. This is a very striking lace and well worth doing, but it will take a long time to produce any useable length of it.

1st Quatrefoil and chain:

With ball and shuttle, R of 5 ds, 3p sep by 5ds, 5ds, cl. *Starting at the base of the last ring, R of 5ds, j to the last p of the prev R, 5ds, 2p sep by 5ds, 5ds, cl.* Repeat twice more. RW. C 5ds, 3p sep by 5ds, 5ds. RW.

1st Trefoil and chain:

R of 5 ds, p, 5ds, j to the middle p of the last ring of the quatrefoil, 5ds, p, 5ds, cl. *Starting at the base of the last ring, R of 5ds, j to the last p of the prev R, 5ds, 2p sep by 5ds, 5ds, cl.* Repeat once more. RW. C 5ds, 5p sep by 5ds, 5ds. RW.

2nd Trefoil and chain:

R of 5 ds, p, 5ds, j to the middle p of the last ring of the last trefoil, 5ds, p, 5ds, cl. Starting at the base of the last ring, R of 5ds, j to the last p of the prev R, 5ds, j to the middle p of the middle ring of the prev trefoil [there are now two trefoils joined by their middle rings], 5ds, p, 5ds, cl. Starting at the base of the last ring, R of 5ds, j to the last p of the prev R, 2p separated by 5ds, 5ds cl. RW. C 5ds, 5p sep by 5ds, 5ds. RW.

3rd Trefoil and chain:

R of 5 ds, p, 5ds, j to the middle p of the last ring of the last trefoil, 5ds, p, 5ds, cl. Starting at the base of the last ring, R of 5ds, j to the last p of the prev R, 5ds, j to the middle p of the middle ring of the 1st trefoil [three trefoils will now be joined by their middle rings], 5ds, p, 5ds, cl.* Starting at the base of the last ring, R of 5ds, j to the last p of the prev R, 5ds, 2p sep by 5ds, 5ds, cl. RW. C 5ds, 3p sep by 5ds, 5ds. RW.

2nd Quatrefoil and chain:

R of 5 ds, p, 5ds, j to the middle p of the last ring of the preceding trefoil, 2p sep by 5ds, 5ds, cl. Starting at the base of the last ring, R of 5ds, j to the last p of the prev R, 5ds, j to the middle p of the 3rd ring of the opposing quatrefoil, 5ds, p, 5ds, cl. *Starting at the base of the last ring, R of 5ds, j to the last p of the prev R, 5ds, 2p sep by 5ds, 5ds, cl.* Repeat once more. RW. C 5ds. RW.

3rd Quatrefoil and chain:

R of 5 ds, j to the last p of the last ring of the preceding quatrefoil, 2p sep by 5ds, 5ds, cl. *Starting at the base of the last ring, R of 5ds, j to the last p of the prev R, 5ds, 2p sep by 5ds, 5ds, cl.* Repeat twice more. RW. C 5ds, p, 5ds, join to the middle p of the chain opposite, 5ds, p, 5ds. RW.

Repeat pattern from 1st Trefoil to 3rd Quatrefoil as many times as needed.

Now study the photo below for the logical conclusion of this procedure. As you can see here the simple trefoil pattern of page 93 has now come full circle, so to speak, by joining the last motif to the first motif of the edging. This creates a six point star pattern often used for snowflakes. One might also manipulate the design to produce four or five point design as well, though it would take slightly more reworking to produce a three point.

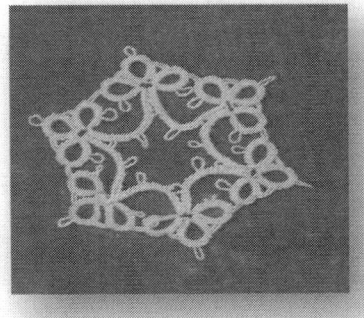

Trefoils Joined into a Six Point Motif

Layering Motifs:

Notice that the design above has an empty space in its center. This need not be so. Layering motives can elaborate a design by making use of such spaces. Almost always this is accomplished by beginning with an innermost motif and adding the second around it. Study the photo below and the pattern following it to see how this is done.

You will notice that the design starts with a center motif that is a six petal daisy with non-joined picots. To this is then added a trefoil edging with chains which joins the bridging chains to each of the successive free picots of the daisy:

Trefoil Design around a Center Daisy

<u>Central Motif:</u>

With shuttle thread, R 5ds, 3 p sep by 5 ds, 5ds, cl. *R 5 ds, j to last p of prev R, 5 ds, p, 5 ds, cl.* Repeat ** 4 more times. R 5 ds, j to last p of prev R, 5 ds, j to first picot of first R (using the double twist as above),[55] 5 ds, cl. Tie threads and cut.

---

[55] See chapter 11 if you've forgotten what this means or how to do it.

Outer Motif:
With shuttle and ball thread, R of 3ds, 5p separated by 3ds, 3ds, close. *Starting at the base of the previous R, 3ds, j to the last p of the prev R, 3ds, 4p sep by 3ds, 3ds, cl.* Repeat between ** once more. RW.[56] Chain 8 ds, j to a free p of the daisy motif, 8ds. RW. R of 5ds, 2p sep by 3ds, 3ds, j to the middle p of the last R of the last motif, 3ds, 2p separated by 3ds, 3ds, close. *Starting at the base of the previous R, 5ds, j to the last p of the last R, 3ds, 4p sep by 3ds, 5ds, cl.* Repeat between ** once.

Repeat the joined trefoil and chain motif around the daisy until the last petal of the last trefoil, then, starting at the base of the previous R, 5ds, j to the last p of the last R, 3ds, 2p sep by 3ds, double twist j to middle p of the first R of the first motif [to finish the circle of the entire motif]. Finish with C of 8ds, joined to the remaining open p of the daisy motif, 8ds, tie to the base of the first R of the first motif.

This type of design is also used commonly as a snowflake.

Repeating and Joining Motifs:

Designs can also be reworked by repeating and joining the same or similar motif, sometimes into three dimensional creations. This was already seen to a limited extent in Lesson 13 when you joined successive daisies edge-to-edge or point-to-point to make an edging.

Study the following photo. Right away you'll notice that it is nothing more than two of the motives shown on page 138. If one joined a similar motif to each of the available free picots of the two, larger and larger projects could be produced. Obviously, there would be fairly sizeable openings between some of them; however, if this was not desired, smaller similar motifs could be centered inside of these openings. Something similar could also be done with the design on page 139.

---

[56] See chapter 9 if you've forgotten what this means or how to do it.

Two Identical Motifs Joined Side to Side

Deciding which patterns to use and how they should be arranged with one another can be done by repeatedly photocopying a single completed motif, cutting out the designs and then arranging them together until you are satisfied with your design.

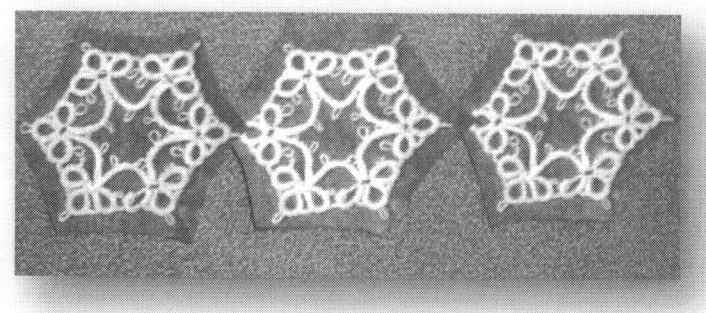

Photocopies of Three Identical Motifs, Point to Point

Photocopies of Five Identical Motifs, Point to Point, leaving Triangular Openings

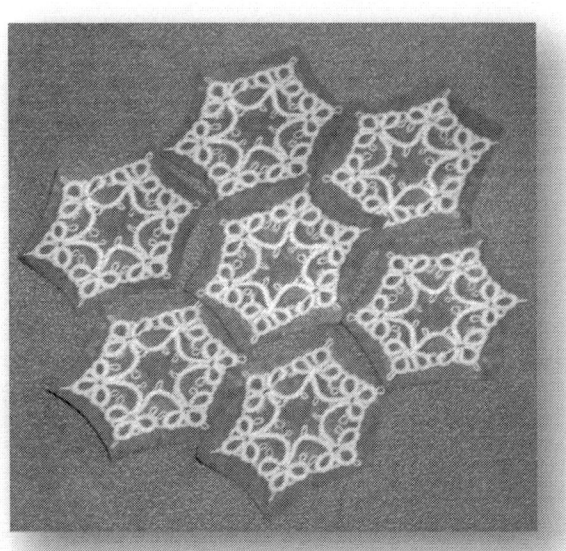

Photocopies of Seven Identical Motifs, Side to Side, leaving Essentially No Openings

Study the photo of the tatted Christmas ornament below.

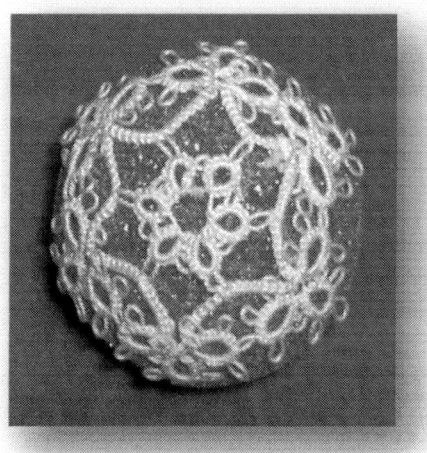

Tatted Christmas Ornament

Although it appears to be different from the other patterns in the book and rather complicated, it is simply two identical motives like those on page 139 joined by matching parts of each by means of their picots. This you already know how to do from previous lessons. This process produces a sort of envelope or pillow form. If all the picots of both are joined, the finished item can be saturated in stiffener and allowed to dry around a balloon inserted between the two motives and then inflated. Once dry the balloon is removed from the ornament.

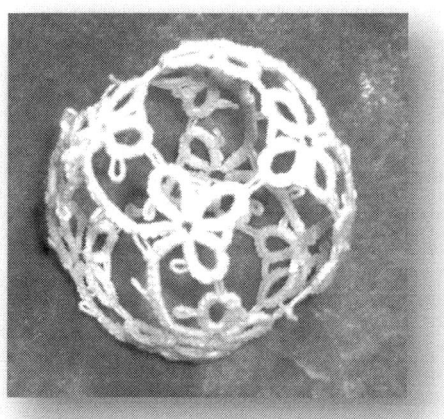

Tatted Christmas Ornament after Stiffening around a Balloon

144

The above ornament is a conjoining of two of the open trefoil snowflakes shown on page 138, as is the following ornament. If you wish to insert a glass or a Styrofoam ball inside the finished form, one pair of the picots of the "envelope" is left unjoined. This leaves a hole large enough for the item to be slipped through it. The two picots are then tied by a ribbon from which the ornament can then be suspended or by the lower curl of a metal ornament hook for the same purpose.

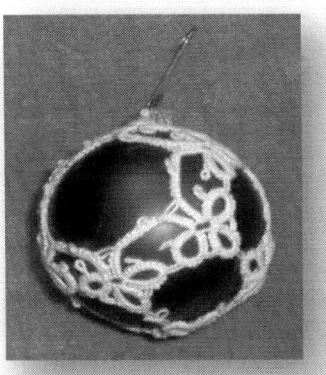

Tatted Christmas Ornament around a Glass Ball

In the case of a Styrofoam ball, the closing picots can simply be pinned in place.

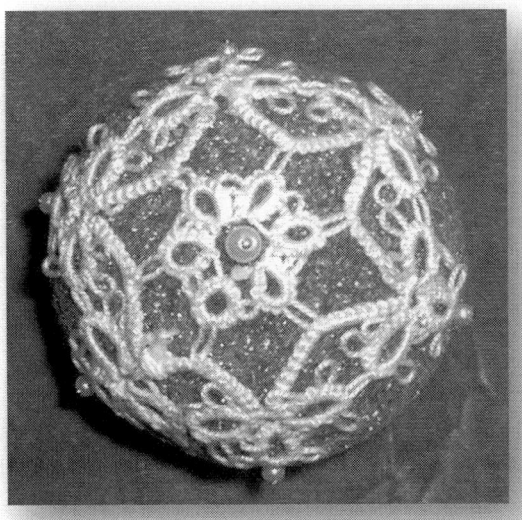

Tatted Christmas Ornament around a Styrofoam Ball with Pins

Using ornamental pins or straight pins through beads, the tatting can be further embellished.

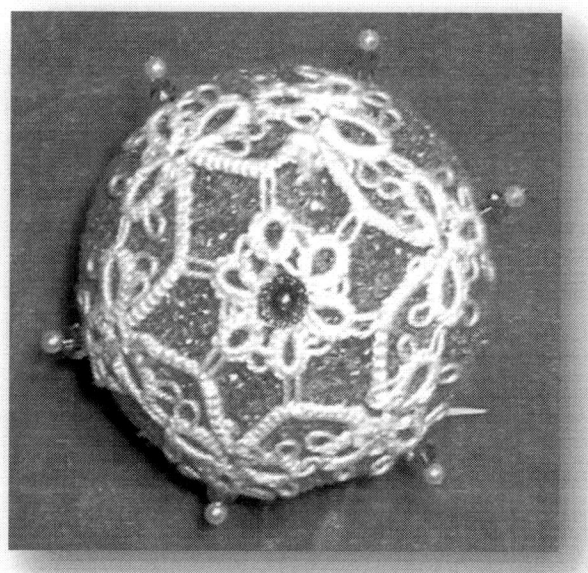

Tatted Christmas Ornament around a Styrofoam Ball with Crystal and Pearl Beads

Repeating forms needn't always be round. Sometimes long narrow motifs similar to the bookmark on page 99 can be altered just slightly to create a motif that can be used either as a medallion, as a Christmas ornament, or in multiples to create a three dimensional form. Below is the bookmark introduced in the earlier lesson.

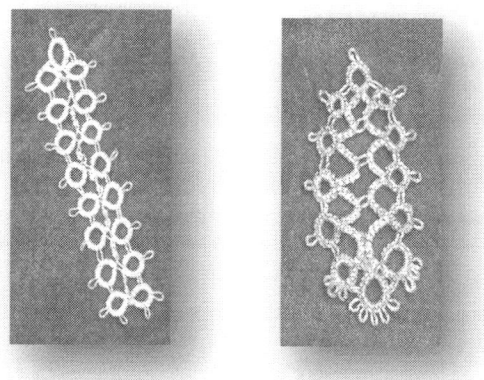

Bookmark and Similar Medallion

By simply working the cascade of rings along the sides in graduated sizes rather than keeping them all the same size, the bookmark takes on a more triangular shape. Adding a large ring with decorative picots to the bottom of the design makes it more closed.

Altered Bookmark Pattern:

Ring 1:   R 5ds, 7p sep by 1ds, 5ds, cl.

Ring 2:   Starting at the base of the prev ring, R 5ds, j to last p of prev R, 1ds, 3p sep by 1ds, 2ds, p, 3ds, cl. Leaving a ½ inch thread space,

Ring 3:   R 4ds, j to last p of prev R, 3ds, 2p sep by 3ds, 4ds, cl. Leaving a ½ inch thread space,

Ring 4:   R 3ds, j to last p of prev R, 3ds, 2p sep by 3ds, 3ds, cl. Leaving a ½ inch thread space,

Ring 5:   R 3ds, j to last p of prev R, 2ds, 2p sep by 2ds, 3ds, cl. Leaving a ½ inch thread space,

Ring 6:   R 2ds, j to last p of prev R, 2ds, 2p sep by 2ds, 2ds, cl.

Ring 7:   Starting at the base of the prev ring, R 4ds, j to last p of prev R, 4ds, 1 large p, 4ds, 1 sm p, 4ds, cl.

Ring 8:   Starting at the base of the prev ring, R 2ds, j to last p of prev R, 2ds, 2p sep by 2ds, 2ds, cl. Weave into the opposite thread space 3 times.

Ring 9:   R 3ds, j to last p of prev R, 2ds, 2p sep by 2ds, 3ds, cl. RW. Weave into the opposite thread space 3 times.

Ring 10: R 3ds, j to last p of prev R, 3ds, 2p sep by 3ds, 3ds, cl. RW. Weave into the opposite thread space 3 times.

Ring 11:   R 4ds, j to last p of prev R, 3ds sep by 1ds, 3ds, p, 4ds, cl. RW. C Weave into the opposite thread space 3 times.

Ring 12: 5ds, j to last p of prev R, 3ds, 3p sep by 1ds, 1ds, j to the 1st p of the 1st ring, 3ds, cl. Tie to the base of the 1st ring.

Any number of rings might be added, so long as the overall shape is tapering rather than vertical, and multiples of these tatted together by means of joins, to make larger motifs: doilies, bells, baskets, and so on.

Chains may be used in place of interweaving to produce a similar result as can be seen in the following photograph and pattern. Notice how similar the two are.

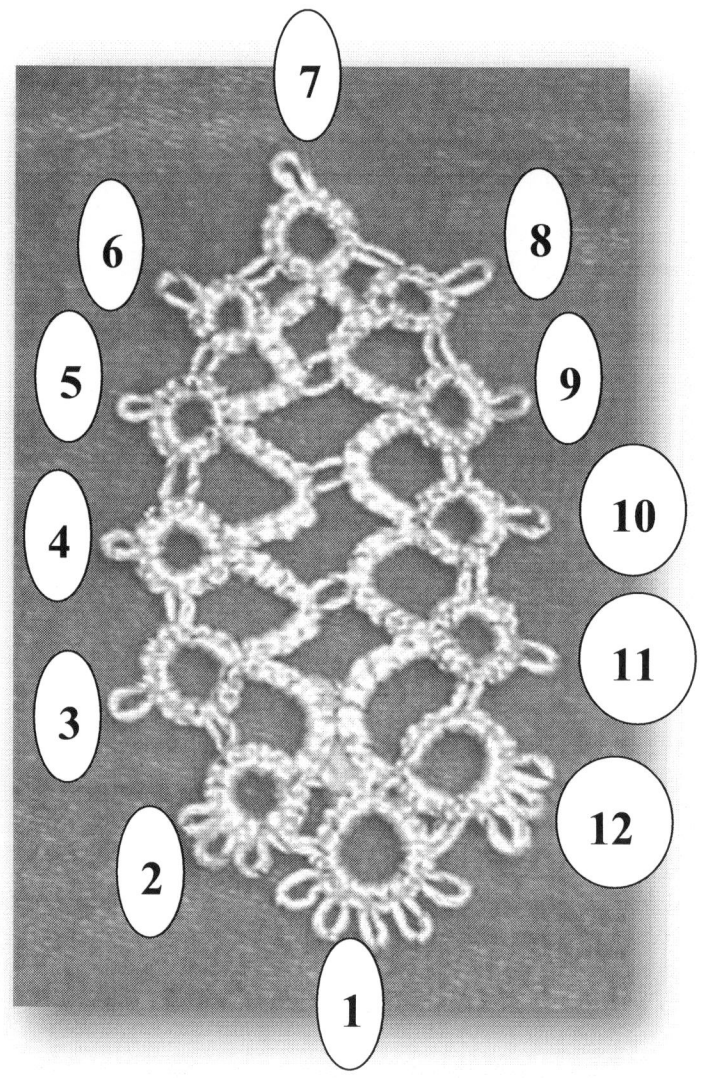

Medallion Variation of the Bookmark

Medallion Pattern (above):

Ring 1: R 5ds, 7p sep by 1ds, 5ds, cl.
Ring 2: Starting at the base of the prev ring, R 5ds, j to last p of

prev R, 1ds, 3p sep by 1ds, 2ds, p, 3ds, cl. RW. C 5ds, p, 5ds. RW.

Ring 3:   R 4ds, j to last p of prev R, 3ds, 2p sep by 3ds, 4ds, cl. RW. C 5ds, p, 5ds. RW.

Ring 4:   R 3ds, j to last p of prev R, 3ds, 2p sep by 3ds, 3ds, cl. RW. C 5ds, p, 5ds. RW.

Ring 5:   R 3ds, j to last p of prev R, 2ds, 2p sep by 2ds, 3ds, cl. RW. C 5ds, p, 5ds. RW.

Ring 6:   R 2ds, j to last p of prev R, 2ds, 2p sep by 2ds, 2ds, cl. RW. C 5ds. RW.

Ring 7:   R 4ds, j to last p of prev R, 4ds, 1 large p, 4ds, 1 sm p, 4ds, cl. RW. C 5ds. RW.

Ring 8:   R 2ds, j to last p of prev R, 2ds, 2p sep by 2ds, 2ds, cl. RW. C 5ds j to the p of the chain opposite, 5ds. RW.

Ring 9:   R 3ds, j to last p of prev R, 2ds, 2p sep by 2ds, 3ds, cl. RW. C 5ds, j to the p of the chain opposite, 5ds. RW.

Ring 10: R 3ds, j to last p of prev R, 3ds, 2p sep by 3ds, 3ds, cl. RW. C 5ds, j to the p of the chain opposite, 5ds. RW.

Ring 11:   R 4ds, j to last p of prev R, 3ds sep by 1ds, 3ds, p, 4ds, cl. RW. C 5ds, j to the p of the chain opposite, 5ds. RW.

Ring 12: 5ds, j to last p of prev R, 3ds, 3p sep by 1ds, 1ds, j to the 1st p of the 1st ring, 3ds, cl.   Tie to the base of the 1st ring.

By joining 5 or 6 of these or similar patterns to one another at the top and sides, and by joining the last made with the first made by means of shared picots, a three dimensional shape is produced. With the opening down, such a pattern produces a bell ornament like that shown below. It can be suspended by a ribbon passed through the top picot with perhaps a large bead or a small bell inside to stabilize it.

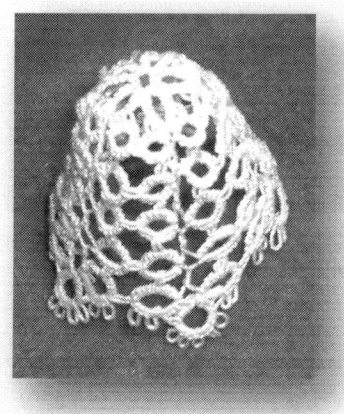

Bell Ornament

With the opening up, it might become a small basket, a ribbon or decorative handle added.

Tatted Basket

To keep their shape, both items need to be molded over a Styrofoam bell shape with an appropriate stiffener, for which see Lesson 16.

Changing Colors:

As noted earlier in the book, a simple change of color within a motif can produce a dramatic effect. This is where the fact that the ball and shuttle threads need not be the same color can produce interesting results with a minimum of effort. The photo on the left below shows a simple design of rings and chains entirely in one color. That on the right shows a change in focus introduced by making the ball thread green and the shuttle thread white.

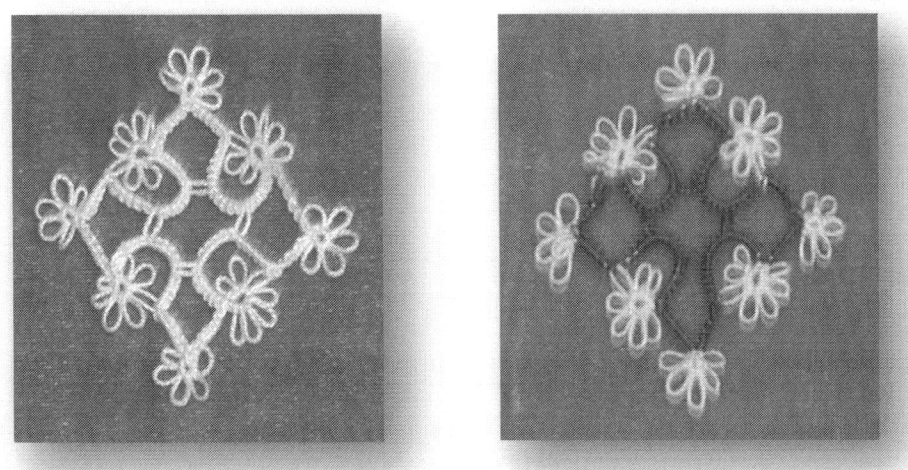

Cross Shaped Motif with Ball and Shuttle Thread White (left) and with Ball Thread Green and Shuttle Thread White (right)

Here again the motif is created by making what is essentially an edging curl around itself by stabilizing it in place with joins.

Pattern:

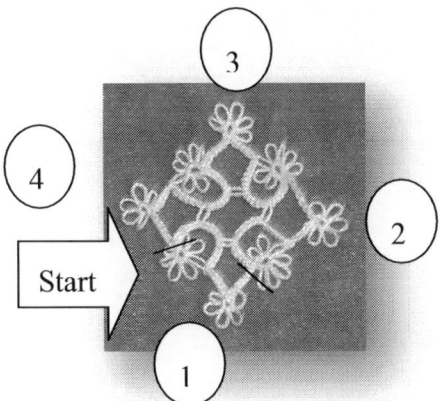

With shuttle and ball threads, and starting as indicated:

151

Corner Number1 (see the diagram): R 1ds, 6p sep by 1ds, 1ds, cl. RW. C 5ds, 2p sep by 5ds, 5ds, j to middle p of the R, 5ds. RW. R 1ds, 6p sep by 1ds, 1ds, cl. RW. C 5ds. RW.

Corner Number 2-3: *R 1ds, 6p sep by 1ds, 1ds, cl. RW. C 5ds, j to second p of the prev chain, 5ds, 1p, 5ds, j to middle p of the prev R, 5ds. RW. R 1ds, 6p sep by 1ds, 1ds, cl. RW. C 5ds. RW.* Repeat between ** a total of two times.

Corner Number 4: R 1ds, 6p sep by 1ds, 1ds, cl. RW. C 5ds, j to second p of the prev chain, 5ds, j to the *first picot of the first chain* [this is a second join in this chain, see the photo], 5ds, j to the middle picot of the prev R, 5ds. RW. C 5ds, j to the base of the first ring. Cut and tie.

The number of double stitches in the chains and/or between the picots of the "flower," as even the number of picots in them, can be altered to suit the needs of your design. Here is a variation on the above motif, using 6 double stitches in the chains and 6 around a single picot in the rings. Study the pattern below to see how it differs from the preceding one.

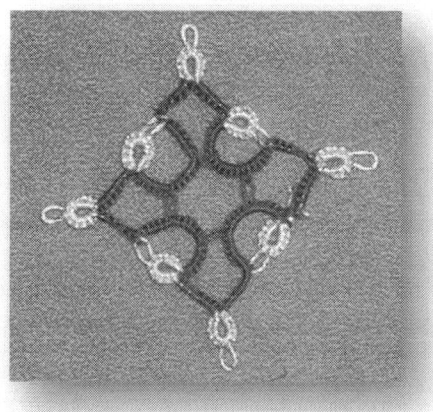

Variation on a Cross Shaped Motif with Ball Thread Green and Shuttle Thread Gold

Variation on the Square Motif:

With shuttle and ball threads,

<u>Corner Number 1</u>: R 6ds, 1p, 6ds, cl. RW. C 6ds, 2p sep by 6ds, 6ds, j to middle 1p of the R, 6ds. RW. R 6ds, 1p, 6ds, cl. RW. C 6ds. RW.

<u>Corner Number 2-3</u>: *R 6ds, 1p, 6ds, cl. RW. C 6ds, j to second p of the prev chain, 6ds, 1p, 6ds, j to middle p of the prev R, 6ds. RW. R 6ds, 1p, 6ds, cl. RW. C 6ds. RW.* Repeat between ** two times.

<u>Corner Number 4</u>: R 6ds, 1p, 6ds, cl. RW. C 6ds, j to second p of the prev chain, then 6ds, j to the *first picot of the first chain* [this is a second join in this chain, see the photo], 6ds, j to the middle picot of the prev R, 6ds. RW. C 6ds, j to the base of the first ring. Cut and tie.

These motives are very similar to the pattern introduced in Lesson 5, where the entire medallion was actually made of chains joined in a similar manner. Because the chains use only reverse work, rather than a change from chain to ring, as a means to create turning points the overall structure is more rounded.

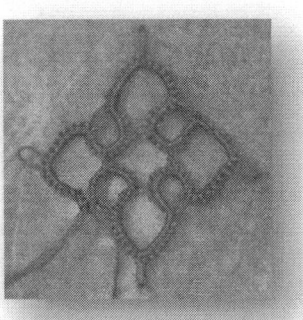

Cross Shaped Motif Entirely of Chains from Lesson 5

Like the trefoil motives used for snowflakes, these can also increase in the numbers of their "points," though more than six can get problematic. Also like the trefoils, these motives may be joined point-to-point or side-to-side with their picots to create larger projects. Below are several arrangements of these medallions.

Photocopied Chain Squares, Side-to-Side

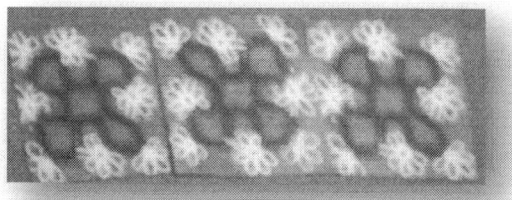

Photocopied Chain and Ring Squares in Two Colors, Side-to-Side

Photocopied Chain and Ring Squares in One Color, Side-to-Side

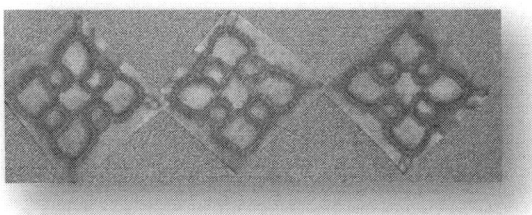

Photocopied Chain Squares, Point-to-Point

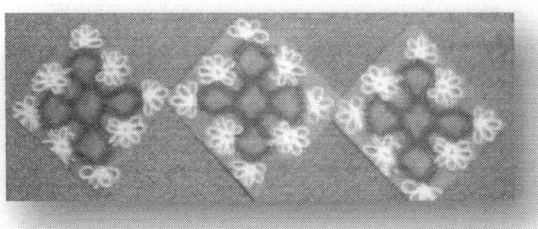

Photocopied Chain and Ring Squares in Two Colors, Point-to-Point

Photocopied Chain and Ring Squares in One Color, Point-to-Point

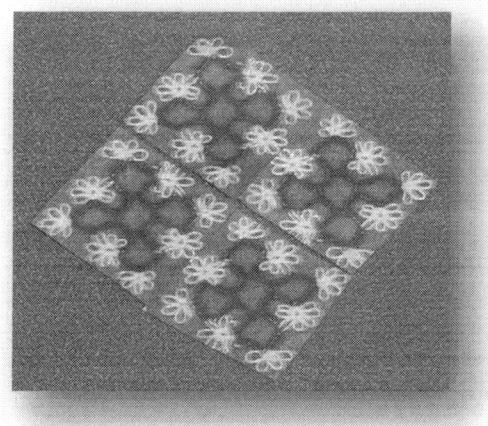

Photocopied Squares in Two Colors, in Blocks

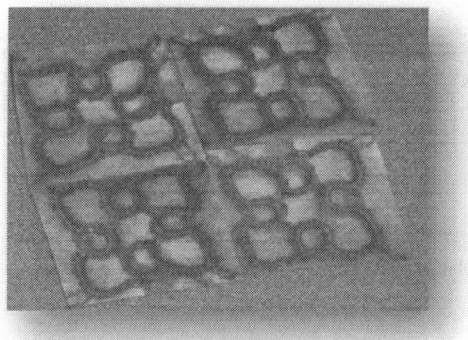

Photocopied Chain Squares, in Blocks

Photocopied Chain and Ring Squares in One Color, in Blocks

Photocopied Chain and Ring Squares in Two Styles, in Blocks

Lesson 15: Reading other styles of pattern instructions

When I first started learning to tat from books of edgings from the 1960s, I found the instructions were all like those I've presented above. In short, included as they were with knitted and crocheted edgings, the instructions for tatted ones were written much as those were, with words and abbreviations.

The first actual book of tatted lace patterns I purchased was a 1988 English edition of a work by Blomqvist and Persson, originally published in Swedish as *Frivoliteter* in 1967. The Blomqvist Persson book presented me with a new format for tatting instructions, and it took me quite a while to get used to them. I assume that the style is Scandinavian or perhaps European in general. The economy of the system is quite remarkable. It uses abbreviations, numbers, crosses and dashes whose purposes are defined at the heading of each pattern. A pattern written for an edging entitled "Ulla,"[57] looking like the photo below, is written:

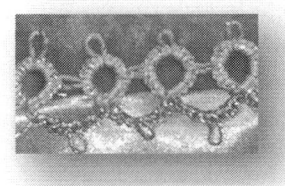

R5-5-5-5. C5-5. R5+5-5-5. C5-5. R 5+5-5-5. Repeat until the lace is the required length.

Here the picot is represented by a dash, the join by a plus sign, a chain by C, a ring by R, and the double stitches by a number. At this level of difficulty the pattern is fairly easily interpreted.

A more complicated pattern instruction in this method is the multiplication symbol. 2x6 by this method, for instance, instructs the tatter to make 2 double stitches, 5 picots separated by 2 double stitches, and 2 double stitches in the method I've employed throughout the lesson book. The "explanation" in the heading is 2x6=2-2-2-2-2-2. The following is from the Blomqvist Persson book:

---

[57] Ibid, p. 22.

Row 1: R 6-5-1. R 1+5-5-1. R 1+5-6. C 16. R 6+5-1. R 1+5-5-1. R 1+5-6. C 16. Repeat until the lace is the required length.
Row 2: +C 2-4-2x7-4-2+4. C 2+4-2x7-4-2+.[58]

This type of shorthand can be very confusing and requires examination of the close-up photos included in the pattern book for verification. Notice the issue with the second row. The locations of the joins are not entirely clear.

In the system I have employed up to this point, the pattern above would read:

Row 1: R 6 ds, 2 picots sep by 5 ds, 1 ds, cl. R 1 ds, j to last p of prev R, 2 p sep by 5 ds, 1 ds, cl. R 1 ds, j to last p of prev R, 5 ds, 1 p, 6 ds, cl. C 16 ds. R 6 ds, 2 picots sep by 5 ds, 1 ds, cl. R 1 ds, j to last p of prev R, 2 p sep by 5 ds, 1 ds, cl. R 1 ds, j to last p of prev R, 5 ds, 1 p, 6 ds, cl. C 16 ds. Repeat until the lace is the required length.

Row 2: Join threads to the center of the first motif of the previous row (apparent only from the photograph). C 2 ds, 2 p sep by 4 ds, 2ds, 7 p sep by 2 ds, 4ds, p, 2 ds, j to the center of the next motif in the previous row (again, only apparent from the photograph included in the pattern book), 4 ds. C 2 ds, j to the last p of the previous chain, 4 ds, p, 7 p sep by 2 ds, 4 ds, p, 2 ds j to the center of the next motif in the previous row (apparent only from the photograph).

While the Blomqvist/Persson book is one of my favorites, it took quite a while for me to interpret some of the patterns in it, and even now when I return to it after an interval of any length I almost always have to reinterpret my chosen pattern. Some of those I've never tried before will still take me a while to work them out—though less time now than it would have. When faced with a pattern of this type, you might like to rewrite it in the system I've shown you above or in a short hand of your own and keep a copy with the original pattern book or with your notes and samples.

More recently I have run into a new approach to writing patterns for tatting. This is a combination of the shorthand method of dashes and numbers

---

[58] Ibid. p. 25.

associated with a schematic of circles and lines showing where rings and chains are located and where picots/joins are located and connected between parts of the motif. Here is an example of the schematic style notation.

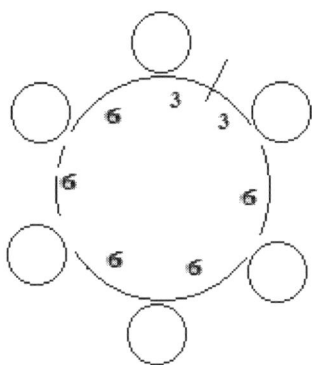

Schematic Drawing of a Tatting Pattern

In written form it would be:

    Ring 3ds, 6p sep by 6ds, 3ds, close.

    This type of pattern book is almost always accompanied by very clear, close-up photos, and I find that the shorthand instructions, the schematics and the photos make the pattern quite clear. This method seems to be the recent trend, so you can anticipate more of this style of pattern book in the future.

Lesson 16: Starching your creations and other ideas.

Most tatted lace benefits from a little starch. A simple spray starch will help picots remain untwisted and well shaped on handkerchief lace and other laces in lighter threads. Sometimes, however, the use of starch can produce very interesting results in other ways. The pattern for a simple doily or coaster when heavily starched can be hung from ribbons or colored threads as window ornaments, for snowflakes on Christmas trees, or on mobiles.

Starched Snowflake on a Christmas Tree

Two identical motifs can be worked or sewn together, saturated in starch, then inflated with a balloon to create round, three dimensional ornaments.

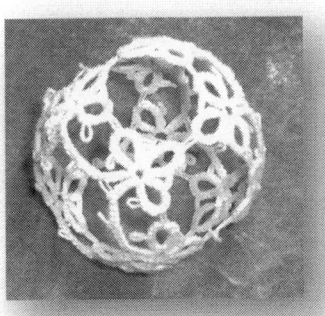

Round Ball Ornament Starched on an Inflated Balloon

By starching two doilies over a box edge to shape them into right angles, and then sewing them to a third, flat doily, a three dimensional snow flake can be created.

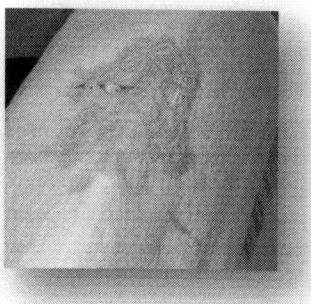

Snowflake Starched on the Corner of a Cereal Box

Starching a doily over a bowl will create a tatted bowl. Stiffly starching and shaping small, round motifs and layering them will produce flowers for bouquets, clothing, and jewelry. An edging can be starched around a bowl or other round object to produce wedding crowns or other head band.

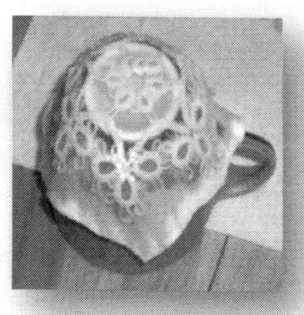 

Snowflake Molded over a Teacup into a Party Favor

Sugar Starch

While there are special starches made specifically for crafting jewelry and other types of objects, a simple laundry starch may be all that is required. One of the easiest and most inexpensive stiffeners, and one that is often ready to hand, is a simple sugar starch, made by mixing equal parts of water and sugar, cooking until clear and cooling before use.

Materials for a Simple Sugar Starch

While it may seem like a good idea, increasing the amount of sugar to make the starch "stiffer" really isn't, since after cooling the sugar tends to crystallize. It's best to use the starch while it is still slightly warm, because the lace tends to take it up less evenly as the liquid cools and becomes more viscous. In this case, the tatted work will have an uneven color, making it look patchy.

Areas of Uneven Starch Saturation

As soon as it is noted, the item should be re-starched with warmer liquid, so it produces a more even appearance.

165

Even Starch Saturation

It is during starching that troublesome picots can be opened out and fixed in place. If they don't remain open after initial placement, they can be fixed open with pins before drying. Note that if you have a lot of picots to pin, you might prefer to place the entire motif over a flat piece of Styrofoam like that used in packing boxes, so that the pins may be placed firmly into the board.

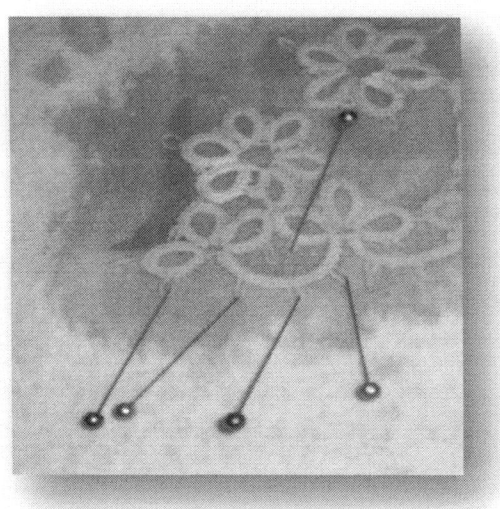

Pinned Piece of Tatting during Starching

Other Stiffeners

White school glue, like Elmer's or Fuller's glue, diluted with a little water so that it easily saturates the tatted work, is also an easy method of stiffening tatted material. In all these cases, the tatted item is saturated with the stiffening medium, then shaped in the desired manner and allowed to dry, either flat or over a mold of some kind. Cleaning is simply a matter of washing the object, which removes the starch and then starching and reshaping it again.

When a more permanent finish is needed, an acrylic spray can be used to stiffen the item, and cleaning is just a matter of rinsing the object in soapy water and allowing it to dry again. This may be a preferred method for jewelry items. In this instance care should be taken to follow the directions of the medium used, particularly that it be used in a well ventilated area.

Generally when tatted motifs are starched and molded, the flat surface or mold is covered with waxed paper, plastic wrap, or baker's parchment to prevent the lace from adhering to the surfaces over which they are dried. This is especially important if using an acrylic finish.

Surface Treatments:

Additional surface treatments can be added either before or after the object is starched. Glitter, sequins or small beads can be lightly glued to the surface of tatted snowflakes, Christmas trees and wreaths.

Ribbon Tie and Pearls Added to an Ornament

Beads and jewelry findings can be added to motifs to create necklaces, earrings, pins, and other items for wear. Ribbons can be woven through tatted edgings for bookmarks, through a pair of round doilies for sachets, or through square motifs to create small gift bags. Below is a list of suggested uses for tatted edgings and motifs.

Segment of Lace Stiffened into a Bridle Crown

Appendices

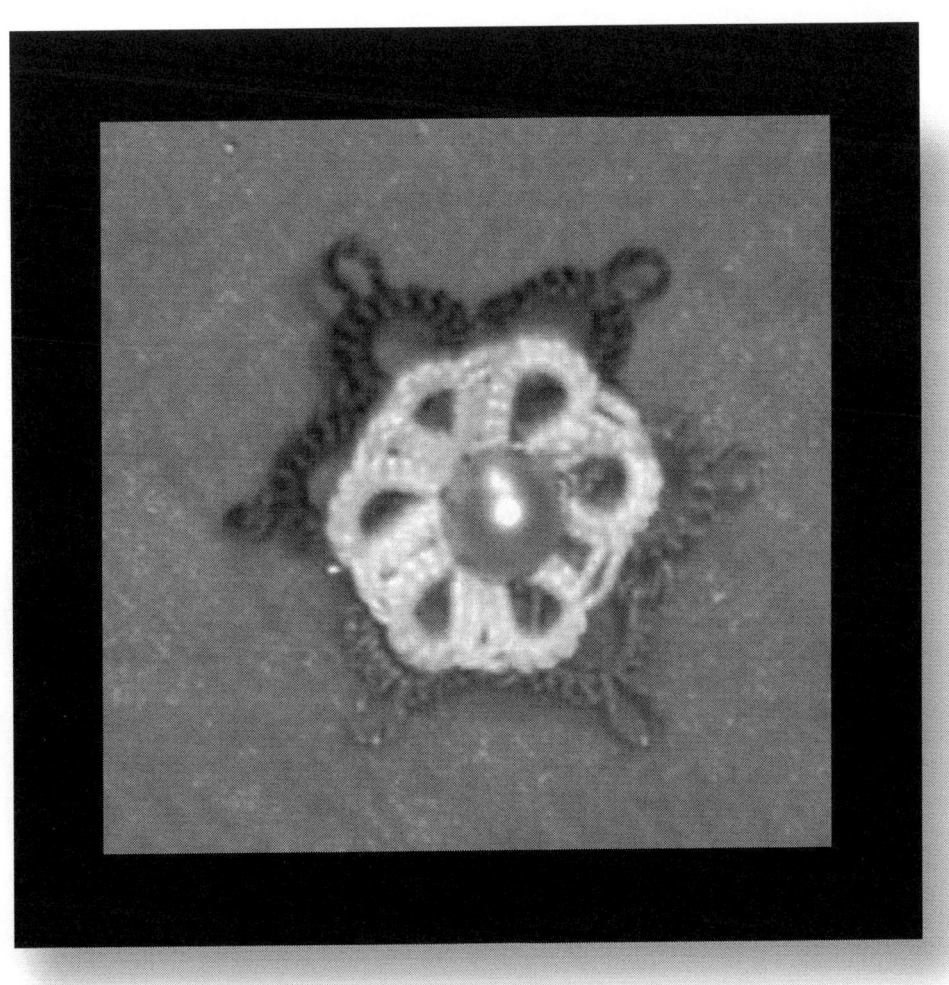

Suggested Uses for Tatted Edgings and Motifs

Bags
Bedspreads
Book illustrations
Bowls
Boxes
Bridal Crowns
Christmas tree trim
Edgings for linens, towels, placemats, napkins, collars, necklines, cuffs, pockets,
Greeting cards
Holiday ornaments
Inserts for table cloths, towels, placemats, napkins, collars, necklines, cuffs, pockets
Jewelry
Lace collars
Lace cuffs
Mobiles
Party favors
Picture frame mats
Purses
Placemats
Rescue covering for spots that can't be removed from a garment
Sachets
Table cloths
Table runners

Decision List: The creative bit

Creativity often boils down to simple decisions or choices. If you have difficulty with the notion of "thinking creatively," use the list below to think in terms of options when you are making a tatted lace project, even if it's a project from a pattern book. By simply making an alternate choice or decision at some or all of these points, your project will be uniquely your own. In fact even without knowing it, you'll be thinking creatively:

Weight/size of thread
Texture of thread—coarseness, metallic shine, etc.
Color of thread
Different colors/textures and sizes of thread on ball and shuttle
Use of beads or focal pendants
Location of beads or focal pendants on ball and/or shuttle thread
Use of joins between rings or motifs
Use of fewer or more picots beyond those for structure
Increase or decrease in the sizes of picots, including stepped or irregular, central or peripheral
Increase or decrease in the number of double stitches between decorative picots
Increase or decrease in the number of rings in a motif
Uniformity or difference in the sizes of rings in a motif
Ring sizes in stepped or irregular character or central rings larger
Use of chains or thread spaces between rings or motifs
Changes in sizes of the motifs in a project that uses several, by adding extra stitches or picots to some motifs and not others,

Tatting Books

Although tatting is not as popular as knitting and crocheting, it still appears in several printed works devoted specifically to tatted designs. Some of these are foreign publications, but the technique is essentially the same. Processing the written instructions is often a matter of interpreting what they are "likely to be," which is itself a matter of experience. Where the language is couched in an unfamiliar script, like Cyrillic, Greek, or Japanese, interpretation will be more problematic. Often pattern schematics are given in such books, which helps. When a foreign tatting book is expensive, it would be best to error on the side of caution, unless you have access to a translator or are very good at interpreting photographs of tatted motifs.

You can sometimes find tatting included in books on other craft techniques, although the section is often a small one. If the patterns are new and interesting to you, the purchase may be worth it. I have a copy of Thérèse de Dillmont's *Encyclopedia of Needlework* which includes tatted designs along with almost every other conceivable handwork. I treasure it.

For those who enjoy second hand bookstores and antique stores that sell old printed matter, you may find tatting included in issues of Coats and Clarks and other booklets and leaflets on the fiber arts dating to the 1930's '40s, and 50's. Women's magazines from these periods also contain tatted and other types of laces, though they become rarer in later decades. I have some of the Coats and Clarks works, and they contain some of my favorite patterns.

Recently some of these older patterns have been collected and republished as "classic" collections. Waldrep's *The Tatter's Treasure Chest* is a recent republication of some of the patterns popular in the 1940s. Most are drawn from The Spool Cotton Company and The American Thread Company. Some of the 19th century works on the subject have been reborn in the form of e-book style publications. I have a Kindle (Amazon.com version of the e-book) publication of *Purse in Tatting and Beads* by Beeton, *Golden Stars in Tatting and Crochet* by Madame Riego de la Branchardière, and *The Bath Tatting Book* by P. P. I tend to find the instructions in these somewhat confusing at times because tatting, like other forms of human endeavor, has evolved over the decades. They are interesting and educational, however, and the experienced tatter should be able to interpret or reinterpret them productively.

Sources for books on tatting can most easily be found on the internet. Some craft stores, like Joann Fabrics and Michaels, may have shuttles and threads but many times do not have books on the subject. Bookstores like Barnes-Noble sometimes have one or two, but the surest source is the internet. A simple Google search will come up with a number of independent craft stores that carry tatting supplies and books: zigzagcorner.com offers a number of English and foreign publications on tatting, for instance, as does hhtatting.com. My favorite source for almost everything is Amazon.com which carries tatting books and supplies and can put you in contact with associates that carry others, sometimes including out of print works. If you have an Amazon Prime membership, you may find some of these items can be shipped for free.

   Another source for tatting patterns may be your public library. Some of the larger public libraries have extensive collections of books on crafts, tatting among them. A simple trip to a photocopy shop will provide you with a collection of specific designs that please you without the cost of entire books on the subject. I have several older patterns which I obtained this way in the 1970's, and I still enjoy them. In fact I laminated them so they would survive my often careless use.

Form for samples and notes

Type Specimen:_____ **Date:**_____

[glue sample here]

Notes regarding thread used.

Pattern Notes (Sources, changes made, uses to which it was put, etc.)

Bibliography

These are some of the books in my collection used to help prepare this publication:

Austin, Catherine. **A New Twist on Tatting**. New York, Sterling Publishing Company: 1994

Baker, Janette. **Learn to Tat**. Berne, American School of Needlework: 2008.

Blomqvist, Gun and Elway Persson. **Tatting Patterns and Designs**. New York, Dover Publications: 1988

Carroll, Janet. **Elegant Tatting Patterns**. New York, Dover Publications: 1996

Coats and Clark's, **Elegant Edgings to Knit, Crochet, and Tat**. Book No. 189. New York, Coats and Clark's, Inc.: 1968.

Coats and Clark's, **Priscilla Edgings**. Book No. 179. New York, Coats and Clark's, Inc.: 1967.

De Dillmont, Thérèse. **Encyclopedia of Needlework**. Mulhouse, France, DMC publications (publication date not given)

Dusenbury, Teri. **Tatting Hearts**. New York, Dover Publications: 1994

Giles, Denise and Kenna Prior. **Ultimate Book of Tatted Doilies**. Big Sandy (TX), Annie's Attic Publications: 2003

Hahn, Monica. **Christmas Angels and Other Tatting Patterns**. New York, Dover Publications: 1989

Linden, Rozella F. **Easy Tatting**. New York, Dover Publications: 1998

Linden, Rozell F. and Barbara Foster. **Celtic Tatting, Knots and Patterns**. Paxton (IL), Handy Hands Publishing: 2004.

Morton, Lyn. **Tatting Patterns**. Lewes (England), Guild of Master Craftsmen Publications: 2002

Nicholls, Elgiva. **Tatting Technique and History**. New York, Dover Publications: 1984

Palmer, Pam. **Tatting**. Princes Risborough (England), Shire Publications Ltd: 2004

Orr, Anne. **Anne Orr's Classic Tatting Patterns**. New York, Dover Publications: 1985

Polachic, Darlene. **Big Book of Tatting**. Berne (IN), House of White Birches Publishers: 2000.

Rogers, Lindsay. **Tatting Collage**. Lewes (England), Guild of Master Craftsmen Publications: 1996

Sunderman, Vida. **Tatted Snowflakes**. New York, Dover Publications: 1995

Waldrep, Mary Carolyn. **Tatter's Treasure Chest**. New York, Dover Publications: 1990

About the Author

Although trained as a registered nurse and working in the field for almost 40 years, Ms Wilson has also been an avid practitioner of a number of the fiber arts, tatting being her favorite. As she says, "It's one of the most portable pastimes I know. If I take a ball of thread and a tatting shuttle in my purse or in my pocket, I'm guaranteed to be patient waiter no matter what the circumstances! It was especially helpful when I lived in Cairo. No one could ever get anywhere quickly or on time, so I usually ended up waiting for friends whenever there was a get together somewhere. Tatting gave me something useful and relaxing with which to occupy my time." When asked if tatting was an "easy" craft to learn, she replied, "It's not easy to learn, especially as it is most commonly taught, but it is easy to do once it is learned. People usually want to start with the rings, but they end up with knots rather than slip stitches. That leaves them frustrated, and they quit. That's why I stress learning with chains first. You learn to see the difference between a knot and a slip stitch right away. Once you've got that, you can go on to rings with much greater likelihood of success."

Printed in Great Britain
by Amazon.co.uk, Ltd.,
Marston Gate.